About the author

CASSANDRA CARTER has been interested in the Western Mystery Tradition for many years. Her areas of study and practice include herbalism, spiritual healing and counselling, earthmagic, Qabalah, and ritual and ceremonial magic. She was born in England, educated in Queensland and has an MA in Medieval Studies from Bryn Mawr College, USA. She now lives in Melbourne, visiting the UK regularly. Not surprisingly, family tradition puts Romany (gypsy) blood into the gene pool, though she works primarily in the Celtic tradition of wisecraft. She has taught Celtic Studies through the Council of Adult Education and has run training courses and workshops in practical magic.

Simple and practical Spells
and Charms to change your life!

every day magic

Cassandra Carter

RANDOM HOUSE AUSTRALIA

Random House Australia Pty Limited
20 Alfred Street, Milsons Point, NSW 2061
http://www.randomhouse.com.au

Sydney New York Toronto
London Auckland Johannesburg
and agencies throughout the world

This Random House Australia edition first published 2000

National Library of Australia
Cataloguing-in-Publication Data

Carter, Cassandra, 1945–

Every day magic: simple and practical spells and charms to change your life!

Bibliography
ISBN 0091 84185 2
1. Magic. 2. Charms. 3. Incantations. I. Title.

133.44

10 9 8 7 6 5 4 3 2 1

Typeset by Midland Typesetters
Printed in Australia by Griffin Press Pty Ltd

Cover and text design by Greendot Design

To Colin
1932–1990
Battledruid, Priest of the God
With whom I first walked the paths of Magic
To Raymond, Priest and Guardian *par excellence*
Beloved friend, partner and fellow-worker in the Light
And with love and gratitude to Dolores and Paddy
Teachers, Keepers of the Faith, Upholders of the Isles of the Mighty
And to the members of Circle Celynen, past and present.

'Thus is the Circle sealed—in Perfect Love and Perfect Trust.'

To dear Paddy

from Cass

St Michael's Day

2000.

contents

foreword

With so many books on the occult and its many variations on sale worldwide now, it is inevitable that comparisons will be made when yet another one appears. However when that one offers finely crafted, well tuned and thought provoking material it is well worth the wait. When it comes from the pen of a knowledgeable, experienced and well-balanced teacher, who knows the value of joy and laughter in the world of magic, it becomes a treasure to keep and return to time and again.

I have had the privilege of working with Cassandra Carter both in ritual and in general occult work for many years. Her discerning mind and total dedication have long been an inspiration to those entering the work of The Mysteries for the first time, and uplifting to those of us who might be described (albeit not within earshot) as The Old Guard!

The hardest part of a book on magic is to strike a balance between what you know and have experienced as a teacher, and what your readers who might well be 'raw recruits' can absorb safely. All too often books on this subject are put onto the market with little or no thought that inexperienced and often very young minds can be given wrong impressions and make wrong assumptions. Those of us who work, teach and write in this field carry a great responsibility for such impressionable minds. Magic in the real sense is not, never has been and never will be Disney's Blue Fairy type stuff! It is purely and simply the application of a science so ancient that its original laws and concepts have long been forgotten. That is why a book like this is important and above all safe to use. Its writer understands the good and bad points of this ancient science, its highs and lows, its benefits and its pitfalls. Let her guide you along old and forgotten paths. She will point out things of interest and value along the way and show you where to put your feet safely. She will bring you to an understanding of a subject to which she has dedicated her life, a life lived with the joy and laughter, tears and sorrow, that all true teachers experience.

One of the most repeated sayings in this kind of work is . . .

'In Perfect Love and Perfect Trust'.

This book was written with this in mind by someone who has lived by those words all her life. Before you lies a journey, tread it with a good heart.

Dolores Ashcroft-Nowicki, 2000.

(Director of Studies of the Servants of the Light and author of books on ritual and ceremonial magic, women's mysteries, Qabalah, Tarot and meditation.)

introduction

Magic is the art of changing consciousness in accordance with will.
Dion Fortune

This is a book about possibilities. Magic—wisecraft—works by and through changing your awareness of what is possible.

So this book is about the ways of causing change. Once you start on this path, change is inevitable. Magic beneficially manipulates change and our response to it so that the outcome is positive.

The book is also about how and why spells and charms work—why certain ways of doing things are effective. Formulas and ingredients are a useful way of focusing the intention, but I believe that if you understand why, say, a love charm contains rose petals, jasmine, seaweed, aventurine, rose quartz and copper, the charm will be more effective.

All the items above are 'under the influence of' the planet Venus, or sacred to Aphrodite, the Greek Goddess of sexual love. If you don't believe in astrology or the Goddess (in which case it's unlikely you'll have picked up this book in the first place) you might prefer to think of them as connecting with the archetypal energy to which the ancients variously gave the name of Aphrodite, Venus, Hathor, Maeve (Medbh) or Freya. In my experience, however, it is easier to connect to the

Goddess on an emotional level than as a faceless archetype. And emotion is the force that empowers a spell.

Emotion is the force that empowers a spell.

Wisecraft—the casting of spells, the making of charms and amulets—is the technology of the Old Religion, the pre-Christian, Goddess-oriented religion of Europe. It works by association and analogy, the principle that 'like calls to like'. That's one reason it's sometimes called 'sympathetic magic'. The belief was that if something looked, or even sounded, like something else, it could stand in its place. It was 'in sympathy' with the original or desired object.

The magics you will find here are simple and available to us all—no conjuring of angels or—Goddess forbid!—demons, no midnight visits to churchyards, no circles of art and triangles of conjuration drawn in chalk or blood and inscribed with mystic runes. If you want to go in for that sort of thing, then the best of luck—you'll need it! However asking the help of angels, archangels and all the company of Heaven certainly has its place . . .

I use the term 'wisecraft' (rather than witchcraft) to refer to the technology of the Old Religion because wise-craft—'making' in accordance with old wisdoms—is what much of the old earthmagic is about.

Wisecraft is the wisdom of our foremothers—our grandmothers and great-grandmothers, and back through many generations. It is a wisdom that has been despised, rejected and thrust into oblivion by the Age of Reason and scientific advances.

I don't decry the advances and advantages of science, medicine, or psychoanalysis. But I would suggest that their tendency has been to disempower us as individuals—to make us believe that we need experts to tell us how to live and what to think and believe.

Wisecraft shows us the way back to our magical true selves. As one of our rituals says: 'We are a part of the Circle of the Wise. There is no mystery that has not already been revealed to us. There is no power we do not already have. We share in all the love there is.'

Wisecraft as I know and practise it uses the materials to hand. If I want or have been asked to make a charm for a particular purpose, I go to my kitchen or the garden or the world at large and see what is available. A sprig of rosemary or mint, a pigeon feather picked up in the street (to give the charm wings to fly free and come home), a pinch of sesame seed (for opening doors—as in Aladdin's Cave), a little sugar to sweeten the outcome—this is kitchen witchery.

Admittedly, my kitchen has a pretty comprehensive array of herbs and spices, but I love to cook, and I have a longstanding interest in herbal medicine, a specific branch of earthmagic. Even hyssop, which I use as an aura cleanser, has medicinal use in the treatment of coughs and colds. But most of the things I will be suggesting are ready to your hand, once you open your eyes and start to look around you.

Recently, a friend was about to have her first child. I was invited to her baby shower, and it was suggested that I might 'do a little ritual' for her. My immediate reaction was that ritual isn't a party game. But I thought about why I'd been asked, and what would be appropriate, given the diverse backgrounds of those attending.

The intention was to give our friend a token of our love and support, something into which we had all put the energy that goes with well-wishing. So instead of words and actions that might have seemed strange or laughable to some of the people there, I kept it simple—always a good rule in wisecraft.

I found a piece of new cloth in my sewing basket. It would make a little pillow or pouch, into which all of us could put a few stitches—locking in our good wishes.

Into the pouch we put rose petals (for Aphrodite), gathered

from the garden and dried in the sun; mugwort (*artemisia vulgaris*, a herb sacred to Artemis, who looks after women in childbirth—the herb is also used medicinally to treat menstrual cramps); an ear of wheat (for Demeter, the Mother Goddess); lavender and camomile, for their calmative effects (lavender from a neighbour's garden, camomile from a tea-bag!); a little tumbled piece of aventurine, a green, jade-like stone which is called the gambler's stone because it is supposed to bring good fortune; and a tiny silver bell (acquired courtesy of a friend's Christmas pudding) as a symbol of celebration and, because of its shape, of the opening womb of childbirth. The ingredients were all readily to hand—even the mugwort had been plucked from a bush I'd walked past a few days earlier.

Our friend went into hospital on schedule and had her baby an hour after admission.

What we had created for her was a *charm*, that is, a physical object into which specific energies or vibrations were put by the use of appropriate herbs and symbols. The word itself derives from an Old French word for a verse said or sung with magical intent—an *incantation* (from the Latin *cantare*, to sing).

I find it useful to distinguish between spells and charms, amulets and talismans.

- A *spell* consists of spoken or written words, defining a magical intention. They are often rhyming, or at least rhythmical, words.

- A *chant or incantation* may also be used (especially in group work) as a means of raising power to focus on a desired outcome. It is distinguished from a spell by being less specific in intent, and because it is sung, or spoken, in a sing-song manner.

- A *charm* is the physical object (like the herb pillow) over which the spell may be spoken and which fixes or holds the magical intent. It is sometimes (in my view, incorrectly) called an *amulet* or *talisman* (both physical objects but of a different form and purpose).

- An *amulet* is a token or symbol, often in the form of a pendant, which is believed by the wearer to have certain powers, often protective. Amulets have a very long history and are often worn by people with no knowledge of wisecraft.

- A *talisman*, in general usage, is the term applied to a good-luck piece. A talisman is written or drawn, on paper, parchment or the appropriate metal, in symbolic language which sets its aim and intent. It is more common in ceremonial magic than in wisecraft.

I shall discuss each of these forms of magic in more detail in Chapter One. For some outcomes, a spell is appropriate; for others, a charm; for still others, an amulet or talisman. Spells and charms are simple, though that doesn't mean they are less effective—on the contrary, because they are often in response to an immediate and urgent need, they are more likely to have the emotional energy that carries them to a successful outcome.

The first rule of magic: words carry energy

The first rule of magic is that words carry energy. Energy is the power to do work. Save energy, think before you speak, and remember that what you say, even in everyday life, has the power to create change.

Marion Weinstein, in her book *Positive Magic*, talks about the ancient Egyptian concept of Ma'Kheru, the Word of Truth. If in everyday life your word is the Word of Truth, if you can be relied on to keep your word and to avoid untruth, then your magical words will carry the force of truth also, and what you say will come to pass.

The converse is also true. If you lie because it's more convenient than the truth, if you make promises you have no intention of keeping ('You must come over' . . . 'Let's do lunch sometime soon' . . . 'Of course I'll help you move house') you undermine magical power.

Say what you mean and mean what you say. At the same time, avoid malice and unkindness. If that means saying nothing, keep silent. In medieval times, this was called 'custody of the lips'. In Buddhism it is one of the Five Precepts and falls under the category of Mindfulness.

Which leads us to the second rule of magic.

The second rule of magic: do harm to none

The second rule of magic is do harm to none. The Law of Threefold Return says that if you use magic negatively—to impair the free will of others, to hurt or to harm—you'll get back what you send out, multiplied by three (at least!) Believe me, this is the kind of instant karma you do not want to invoke! The Law of Threefold Return is particularly relevant to love magic and protective magic, and I'll deal with it in more detail in those chapters. But it's also relevant to the way you deal with people in everyday life. Like calls to like, love to love, and ill will to ill will.

If you are unkind, bitchy, given to malicious gossip, then those negative energies will in due course bounce back to make your life as unpleasant as you have made other people's. If you consciously try, however, to have a smile and a pleasant word for those you meet and work with, your personal as well as your magical life will benefit enormously. 'Do unto others as you would have them do unto you' is sound magical practice.

It's also something to bear in mind should you have a grievance (for example, you think someone is illwishing—hexing—

you) and you decide you want revenge. It's much more effective to return any negative magic to the sender (see Chapter Six for techniques) than to try to hex them in turn. For one thing, you may well be wrong about the source of your 'bad luck'. And even if you're right, the karmic consequences of using negative magic will reverberate, not just through this life, but through lives to come.

If negative magic is your thing, stop reading now and look for another book. And make sure that you're very, very well-trained and make no mistakes, because the masters you will serve have nil tolerance for failure.

The third rule of magic: define your terms!

The corollary of the first and second rules is define your terms! You need to think carefully and clearly about outcomes before working even an apparently simple spell.

There is a lovely story about the wife of an eminent occultist who decided she could use this magic stuff for the practical purpose of getting herself a winter coat—the present one being, she felt, past its use-by date. So she worked a ritual accordingly (without consulting her husband, who, she thought, would not approve of such a use of high magic). And the winter coats did indeed start to arrive—fifteen in all, from various donors. They were the wrong size, the wrong colour, in an unbecoming style, some so secondhand that they made her current coat seem positively new. When her husband stopped laughing, he explained that she should have been absolutely specific in what she required—and that it would have been much simpler if she'd just told him she needed a new coat!

If your intention is not clear, your object not well-defined, then there is no straight path for the magic to take. At the least, it will dissipate and you'll have wasted your time. At the worst, it may double back and bite you in the bum!

The Cosmic Wet Fish Factor

In my classes I have called this double-back the 'Cosmic Wet Fish' factor—the Lords of Karma will beat you around the head and body with a wet fish (as in the Monty Python skit) to teach you not to do whatever it was. Fortunately they're a forgiving lot. If you acted out of ignorance rather than malice or ill will, the lesson is likely to be quite gentle and often funny—like working for a lot of gold and being given a tankful of goldfish. And you'll be given a chance to make good any damage you may have inadvertently caused.

I speak about the Gods, the Lords of Karma, and so on, but earthmagic does not require a religious context *per se*. Any of the charms and spells I suggest can be performed without reference to any deity, although there must be emotional energy (desire) to empower them. My own experience, however, is that working within a spiritual framework gives access to archetypal powers which are, quite literally, para-normal. But the Powers may be the Greek gods, the Celtic pantheon, the sephiroth on the Tree of Life. Or they may have the names of Christian saints or the cardinal Archangels. The Goddess may for you wear the face of the Blessed Virgin; you may sanctify your charms by the power of the Holy Spirit; your spells may be prayers.

Magic is magic. But the frame of reference may vary.

And ultimately the magic is in you—not in spells and charms, words and things. They simply help you focus your intent on the desired outcome. Ultimately, magic isn't something you do. It's something you are, at every waking and sleeping moment. It breathes with your every breath. It is found in the way you live, the things and people and animals that surround and support you. Cooking can be a magical act. So too, can setting a bowl of flowers or fruit on a table, lighting a candle, pouring a glass of wine.

Intention is all.

Chapter One

first catch your dragon...

When you open a cookbook about, say, Thai or Indian food, there will always be a section on special ingredients and equipment you will need if your food is to taste authentic. It will never taste quite as it does in Thailand or India because the vegetables grow in a different soil, the herbs and spices may be more or less fresh, and so on. But if you've used the right equipment and ingredients, the results should taste as good. Because of the high quality of ingredients available here, the end result may even be better. This section is the equivalent of a chef's *batterie de cuisine* and will tell you what you really need for successful spellcasting, amazing amulets, terrific talismans and charged-up charms.

'Eye of newt and toe of frog . . . '
William Shakespeare, *Macbeth*

Some spells or charms, especially those taken from old *grimoires* (magical recipe books) have ingredients that seem bizarre, distasteful or simply unobtainable. Dragon's blood, snake's tongue, mousetail, Jew's-ear ... The most famous is probably Shakespeare's 'eye of newt and toe of frog' formula in *Macbeth.*

The passage has a quite different dimension when you realise that the ingredients are being given their common, regional or dialect name—in the way that, for instance, *artemisia vulgaris* is called mugwort because it was used as a bitter to flavour beer.

The ingredients in the witches' cauldron have various uses, but the greater proportion of them are in fact hallucinogens, and are readily absorbed through the skin. The recipe may well be based on one for the so-called 'Flying Ointment' which the witch-trials claimed witches rubbed on their broomsticks in order to hitch an easy ride to the nearest Sabbat (festival). The witches in *Macbeth* could, in modern parlance, be said to be having a really heavy trip on bad acid!

So if you're asked to use lamb's tongue or bachelor's buttons, don't go to a butcher or a menswear shop (or snaffle a passing bachelor, though acquiring the buttons could be fun!), but instead try your garden or a herbalist's.

And so to 'Dragon's Blood' and whether you actually need to set a dragon-trap to obtain it.

You may have seen this substance in a recipe, or in a shop selling spellcraft materials. It's a reddish powder, usually sold in small packets at reasonable prices—much more reasonable than if a passing dragon had actually donated a pint or so of best ichor to your magical intent. It's the resin of a tree found in South-East Asia, *daemonoropis draco*, species *dracaena*. Hence the name of the powder—the Latin for dragon is *draco*. Non-magically, it's used to colour violin cases with that lovely reddish hue. In magic, it is used in spells or talismans of protection, where it is added to or used as the ink in which the spell or talisman is written. It can also be added to incenses serving the same purpose.

So what do you do if you want to make a protective charm and you're fresh out of Dragon's Blood? You use commonsense and a suitable substitute, worked out according to something called a table of correspondences.

This goes with that: the Doctrine of Correspondences

Correspondences have nothing to do with how to write a thank-you letter and a great deal to do with practical—and sometimes impractical—magic.

In my kitchen is a glass jar labelled 'Dragons' Toenails', the contents of which I have used in protective charms. It contains the small, very hot dried red chilis used in Thai cooking. The name is courtesy of a friend's young daughter who saw the unlabelled jar and said 'Cass, they look like dragons' toenails.' She had an instinctive understanding of one of the rules of this kind of magic: like calls to like. If something looks like another thing, it can very often be used as its substitute. The technical magico term for this is 'the Doctrine of Correspondences'.

There are books around which will give page after page, table after table of planetary attributions, herbs, spices, gemstones, colours, perfumes, incenses, Qabalistic sephiroth (the stations on the Tree of Life representing various stages of manifestation of the Creator—see Glossary), Tarot major (and minor) arcana cards . . . It doesn't have to be that complicated (though if you enjoy Trivial Pursuit, it can be quite good fun). I have listed some of the more useful titles at the end of the book.

The principle is simple. Magical ingredients are generally organised in categories according to the Four Elements (Earth, Air, Fire, Water) or the planets (including for this purpose the Sun and the Moon).

So, back to our protective charm.

We are told that Dragon's Blood is used for protection. Why? I would think it is because of the colour it has and gives. The colour associated with protection (and courage) is red. It is the colour of blood, dragonish or human. The red coats of the British Army, the Red Flag of Courage, have the same kind of association. It's also the colour associated with the element of Fire and the planet Mars. So: what's red and has a fiery energy? How about chili pepper? Add a dash of Tabasco to your red ink. (But don't add chili powder to an incense unless you want to clear the space of all human and animal, as well as astral, life forms—it's the nearest thing to tear gas outside a baton charge.)

It makes perfect sense in wisecrafting terms. After all, Great-Granny Smith didn't say to herself, 'I must pop down to the apothecary and pick up a packet of Dragon's Blood so I can protect Johnnie when he takes the pigs to market.' (And she probably wouldn't have had access to chili pepper either, come to think of it.)

But she looked around her kitchen and her garden and plucked a sprig of rowan or rosemary, binding them into an equal-armed cross with a bit of red thread. Or she just thought about a Spell of Going and Returning, and taught Johnnie the words to say as he travelled. Simple, but effective wisecraft.

Granny knew, because she'd learnt from her mother or from the village wisewoman, which plants were protective, just as she knew that mugwort tea eased menstrual problems. She would have neither known nor cared about the planetary influences or the deities associated with the remedies. Indeed, she may well have considered herself to be a good Christian and condemned such things as 'heathenish'—quite appropriately, since the word means 'of the heath', just as 'pagan' is derived from *paganus*, a country-dweller.

But we have lost that inheritance and must rediscover or rebuild it if we want to walk the old ways. This book aims to give you some signposts on the path.

Spells, charms, talismans, and amulets: which and when?

SPELLS

'Spell' is often used as the generic name, a kind of shorthand for different types of natural magic. As I said in the Introduction, I prefer to distinguish between spells and charms, although of course the two may be used together and often are—the spell being used to *charge* or activate the charm once it is assembled.

A spell is by definition verbal—it uses words, though they may be spoken or written. In our society we are probably likely to write or compose a spell before speaking it. In our foremothers' day, when literacy was less common and poetry or verse more of a spoken art, a spell would have been put together on the spot, as needed.

And this gives a useful clue to the function or purpose of a spell. It was originally voiced in response to an immediate and pressing need—for help, protection, or a domestic or personal crisis.

The equivalent in the Christian tradition is a fervent prayer: 'God help me!', 'Angels guard me as I sleep', 'Blessed Mother, watch over me'.

A spell asks for immediate action. The trick here is to define what sort of action, or more accurately, what sort of result you're aiming for. A general cry for help will always be answered. Indeed, there is a rule that Them Upstairs are not permitted to intervene in human affairs unless help has been asked for. But the help may not quite be in the form you were expecting, or hoping for. Sometimes the Goddess, like any good mother, gives us not what we think we want, but what we truly need.

The fourth, or possibly the first and foremost, rule of magic: be prepared to adjust your vision to take advantage of what is offered. It may be better than you'd hoped.

There are no setbacks, only unrealised opportunities.

You may be tired of your job and decide you need a holiday. You devise a spell accordingly, for example:

What I need is a holiday
A break from all this trouble and fuss
Give me a fortnight somewhere warm
So I don't have to catch my daily bus!

What you get is not a fortnight on the Barrier Reef, all expenses paid, but a fortnight off work with a nasty bout of flu. But you are warmly tucked up in bed, you don't have to go in to work—and you also get time to think about where you are going. Does your job truly fulfil you or simply provide a means of meeting the bills? If the latter, what can or should you be doing about it? Do you need to change jobs, or take a course to give you better qualifications? Maybe what you need is another area of fulfilment. Paint, write poetry, take up study in a field totally unrelated to the way you earn a living, like Tarot or aromatherapy.

What the spell has given you is space to consider your options—and the drive to do so, which would probably not have been there if you'd simply blissed out on sun, surf and beach boys. So when you think a spell hasn't worked, take another look at what's happened to cause change in your life, and what unrealised opportunities you may be ignoring.

So: spells are word-magic. Any effective public speaker uses word-magic, as do actors, good salespeople, hypnotherapists and poets, to name but a few.

The earliest and oldest magic was the naming of things. It was believed that to know a person's (or a god's) true-name gave the knower power over the known. So in some cultures a person has a public name (the name used in everyday life); a private name (the name, often a nickname or pet name, given by family or friends and used in intimate situations or solely within the family); and the true-name, known only to the person and perhaps his or her spiritual guide or mentor—and, of course, to the Gods.

In some magical traditions the new initiate takes a Circle, Coven or Lodge name or motto by which they are known within that group. Dion Fortune, a leading occultist of her time (1890–1946) took her writer's name from her Lodge motto, 'Deo non Fortuna' ('to God not Fortune'). Such names express a magical intent or focus, or place the initiate under the guidance and protection of a deity or archetype—just as a Catholic will have a saint's name and celebrate the saint's feast as their name-day.

These names are a kind of spell, and should be chosen with care. Caitlin Matthews, in *Voices from the Circle*, tells an amusing but cautionary story about choosing Rhiannon as her tutelary goddess. In Celtic tradition, Rhiannon is the sweet singer whose birds so enchant the soul that it forgets time and place and moves wholly into the realm of Faerie. Caitlin is an enchantress in the old sense of the word, with a singing and speaking voice of great beauty, hence her choice of Rhiannon. But as she says ruefully, what she forgot was that in the Mabinogion Rhiannon is also the Bearer of Burdens, and Caitlin spent a number of years thereafter bearing a variety of burdens, personal and emotional, that she hadn't counted on as being part of the deal.

Once again: words have power. Words *are* power. Choose them and use them with care.

So, having defined your aims and objectives, and spent some time finding exactly the right words, what next? There are several options.

- You can say the words, once, with all the emotional force and power you can muster. It's helpful to prepare the space and focus yourself before doing this: see Chapter Two.

- You can set them to music and sing them.

- You can use them, if they're brief and to the point, as a kind of mantra and spend, say, nine or thirteen minutes (nine is the number associated with the Triple Goddess and thirteen is the number of lunar months in a year) repeating them as an endless chant (in the way that the Buddhist *om mani padme hum* is used).

- Or you can write the spell down using the appropriate coloured ink and paper (see Chapter Three), carry it around next to your skin for a day, and then burn it—for preference, on a new or a full moon (see Chapter Eight). The burning releases the energy of the spell to do its work—analogous to the release of the 'cone of power' at the culmination of group work.

Then—and this is the hard bit—*put it out of your mind.*

'Acting in Accordance'

The more often you think 'Oh, it hasn't happened yet', the more you disempower what you've done. There's a principle called 'acting in accordance' which I first came across in *The Act of Will*, a book on psychosynthesis, where it is used in reference to depressive states. Roberto Assagioli, the author of the book, says that if we are depressed, it is almost impossible to change how we feel by an act of will—it is like trying to pull yourself up by your shoelaces. But if we act *as if* we are cheerful, as if the Universe is benevolent and life is good, gradually the inner reality will accord with the outer face, and we will become as happy and fulfilled as we pretend.

So too in spellcraft. Spend time and energy focusing on what it is that you want to manifest, get the words just right, add the caveat 'For the good of all and according to the free will of all': then release the spell to do its work, and act *as if* the desired outcome has already come to pass.

'For the good of all and according to the free will of all'

I learnt this invaluable phrase from Marion Weinstein's *Positive Magic*. Attach it to all your spells, charms or whatever as a kind of 'amen'. It is a very simple way to avoid the Cosmic Wet

Fish factor, the karmic comeback if your motives weren't quite as pure as you thought.

It also doesn't negate the spell or charm, but provides an avenue for the Powers to operate in ways that you may not have foreseen.

You may be thinking, for example, of devising a love spell. There is someone at the office to whom you are very attracted. You think you have a lot in common, but he doesn't seem to know you exist, except as a colleague. If you can only attract his attention he'll see you are meant for each other.

But having read this far, you might (I hope) be a little more cautious about what you aim for. You think about this man, what's attractive about him. Well, he's nice-looking. But he also seems to have a really warm, friendly personality. He makes you, and others in the office, feel good when he's around. You decide it's that warmth, the sense of being cared about and for, that makes him special.

So you set to work on your spell. You don't name the man in the spell (very bad karma—see Chapter Four). But you define those qualities that attract you. You want someone who's good-looking, who is warm and loving, and makes you feel warm and loved and cared for, who's devoted to you. You find the right words, finish with 'for the good of all and according to the free will of all', and release the spell to do its work.

A few days later, your parents give you a dog—a handsome golden retriever. He's warm, and loving, and totally devoted to you. Are the Gods having a joke? (They do have a sense of humour!) You smile, and shrug, and thank them.

Dogs need exercise. You take your new friend for a run in the park—and who should you meet but your office colleague, also walking a dog. You both have a reason to get talking—animals are great ice-breakers. And he has noticed you, as you'd originally hoped. Whether a romance develops is now up to the two of you—and maybe your two dogs!

For the good of all, and according to the free will of all. Memorise that phrase!

But what if the desired outcome is more complex and the 'instant fix' of word-magic doesn't feel appropriate—for example, you've just acquired a new car and you want it to carry you safely wherever you need to go? In other words, the need is ongoing (some love charms fall into this category, if what you want is true love, not lust, for example).

This is where charms, amulets and talismans come into their own. They are objectifications, in the physical world, of your desire. They usually require more energy in their preparation than a simple spell. Herbs need to be gathered, with reference to the appropriate correspondences. An amulet needs to be made or acquired, and cleansed before being charged with your intent. Talismans need to be researched, parchment and ink obtained, and the talisman drawn before it is empowered.

So are they worth the extra effort, and which do you choose for your purpose?

CHARMS

A *charm* is a collection of herbs and other objects (e.g. tumbled stones, symbols like a bell or a heart) chosen for their appropriateness to the desired outcome according to the Doctrine of Correspondences (see table below). These are tied or sewn into a piece of new cloth and then *charged* using a spell or (better still) a chant.

The cloth must be new so that it carries no psychic or astral vibrations from its previous use, unless this is consciously desired. For instance, if you were making a healing charm, tying it in fabric previously worn by the intended recipient will help the blessing home in on its target.

Generally speaking, you'll want to use new cloth. Silk is often favoured. It is traditionally held to be a psychic insulator, i.e. it prevents the entry of negative vibes, which is why it's used to wrap Tarot cards and magical tools such as the *athame* (the ritual blade). Logic, however, says to me that if silk is capable of keeping out negative vibes, it must also be capable of keeping in magical vibes: which is really counterproductive in charm work.

I use and recommend pure linen or cotton (if you can find it), or the felt squares available in fabric or handicraft shops. These come in an assortment of colours (see Chapter Three), are inexpensive and easy to store and handle; and they're a natural fibre. Avoid synthetics. Choose the colour appropriate to the charm (or use white, which contains all colours), put the selected herbs and objects inside, and sew into a pillow or tie into a pouch or bundle (like an old-fashioned Christmas pudding).

If you're using the tying method, choose cord or thin ribbon appropriate to your intent, or use gold or silver thread. The knots should be a propitious number—nine is always a good bet. It is the number attributed in Qabalah (the name given to the Jewish system of magic and mystical teachings, see Glossary) to the sephira *Yesod*, associated with the Moon and the Triple Goddess. But for an abundance charm, four knots (Jupiter), or possibly ten—the number associated in Qabalah with *Malkuth*, the earth plane. For a love charm, tie seven knots, or use copper wire (both associated with Venus/Aphrodite)!

The completed and charged charm should be put or carried in an appropriate place: the car safety charm hanging from the mirror or put under the driver's seat; a love charm carried on your person. I have an abundance charm tucked under my computer monitor as I write this.

Spellboxes have recently become a popular way of packaging a charm. They have their uses, though they're a bit tricky to tuck in your bra—the appropriate place to carry a love charm! And I like to handle a charm, work it in my hands, massage it a bit to zap up the energy. This is difficult with a spellbox. You can also find yourself running out of shelf or altar space as the boxes mount up, especially since you shouldn't re-use a box once the spell has done its work. And if it's attractive enough to serve as a spellbox, you'll want to keep it!

A more useful function for a spellbox is to keep the ashes of written spells that have been sent on their way by burning. Throw the collected ashes into the Samhain (Celtic New Year, All Hallows Eve) bonfire at the turn of the year (see Chapter Eight).

AMULETS

An *amulet* is a single (as opposed to a compound) object chosen for its suitability to the purpose and specifically dedicated and charged for that purpose. It is usually worn on the person, often as a pendant.

The pentagram is an amulet as well as a profession of faith, that is, if it has been magically charged and dedicated to the work of protecting its wearer. The Saint Christopher medal hanging in your car is an amulet invoking the protection of the Saint of travellers. The acorn, sacred to Zeus, was believed to give protection against being struck by lightning. The four-leafed clover is thought to bring good luck, as is the rabbit's foot (though not to the rabbit!).

Amulets are most commonly protective in function. Amongst the most frequently seen are:

- The **star**—five-pointed (the pentagram), the symbol of the Goddess and of the Four Elements governed by Spirit; six-pointed (the hexagram, Star of David or Seal of Solomon), representing the magical principle 'as above, so below'; or seven-pointed (associated with Inanna and with the sephira Netzach) and used as an amulet to attract love.

- The **cross** or crucifix; the equal-armed Cross of the Elements.

- The **holy medal**. The Saint Christopher medal is probably the most common. A Michael medal, if you can find one, is useful on several levels, but especially as a protection against ill will—I was buying them by the dozen at one stage! Not, I should add, for myself, but for good Catholics concerned about malocchio (the evil eye).

- The **ankh** (calling on Isis as the Great Mother), a symbol also of eternal life.

- The single **blue bead** (sometimes with a small black dot representing the pupil) which gives protection against the evil eye. It's Middle Eastern, often Islamic, and may be combined with the *Hand of Fatima*.

- The **Eye of Horus**—Ancient Egyptian. Horus was the son and protector of Isis. Often worn by men who wish to indicate their desire to serve the Goddess as protector of women, who are Her garments.

- **Thor's Hammer**—for men working in the Norse tradition, as a symbol of the God; and for women of that tradition who wish to put themselves under the God's protection.

Crystals and other tumbled stones (rose quartz, turquoise, carnelian) are very useful as amulets, especially since they are easy to charge with magical intent. The colour of the stone is a useful guide to its magical function (see Chapter Three).

But you can also make or obtain an amulet to attract love, or money, or health. Paul Beyerl, author of *The Master Book of Herbalism*, suggests using a small leather bag (a Mojo bag—see Glossary) to hold the appropriate herbs and other objects: in effect, a long-lasting charm in a form suitable to carry or wear.

What makes any of these things an amulet, as opposed to merely a pretty or curious object to hang around your neck, is the act of imbuing it with magical intent—directing its function and purpose. I will suggest specific amulets in the relevant chapters.

TALISMANS

Talismans have some similarities to both charms and amulets. The difference, as I understand it (and other people, such as Robin Skelton in *Talismanic Magic*, use different definitions) is that a talisman is written or drawn (on paper, parchment, or the appropriate metal) using symbolic language (especially Hebrew or Latin) and pictorial representation to focus its intent.

Talismans are often consecrated in the names of archangels deemed to have specific responsibility in the area on which the talisman is focused—a kind of celestial Public Service with various departments headed by an archangel who in turn delegates tasks to a squadron of angels, each squadron having a name by which it is invoked and through which the archangelic power is delegated.

If this sounds complicated, it is. When you take on board the teaching that each angel has its particular hour of a particular day of a particular month, and that talismans have an appropriate metal, gemstone, incense, flower and colour, depending on their purpose, you'll understand why I personally prefer spells, charms and amulets.

On the other hand, calling on the angelic powers has a fail-safe factor. It is said that angels cannot do any work contrary to the will of the Most High. So if your intention is self-serving or not in the interests of all parties, the talisman simply won't work—and you will be prevented from falling into sin.

There are other and simpler ways to avoid the Cosmic Wet Fish factor. Add that useful phrase 'for the good of all and according to the free will of all' to your spells and other work—just as effective and considerably less complicated!

But if your path is ceremonial, talismans may well be for you. Don't let me dissuade you. Robin Skelton's *Talismanic Magic* is a comprehensive guide to the subject, and will also introduce you to the delights of various magical and angelic alphabets.

The advantage of talismans (as I define them) is that they can easily be carried on your person (for an intention affecting the self), in a wallet (for a money talisman), or put under your pillow (to affect your dreams and increase intuition and contact with the High Self, sometimes called your Holy Guardian Angel). They should be wrapped in black silk once they have been charged (i.e. imbued with magical power), and should be destroyed (usually by burning) once they have achieved their purpose.

Ingredients and how to choose them

I have given the planetary areas of influence in a table below. In each chapter devoted to a particular subject (e.g. abundance, love, protection) I will list the herbs, gems, colours and metals appropriate to that kind of work. Once you have decided on the relevant planetary influence, one herb can do the work of another (see my comments on Dragon's Blood and chili pepper) unless specifically stated otherwise.

It's only ceremonial magic that insists that in order to invoke the protection of Isis the magician (as well as being appropriately dressed in blue and silver) must use, say, kyphi incense, fresh lotus flowers and clean silver sand from the banks of the Nile, and work only on a Friday! Wisecrafters simply say 'Lady Isis, cover me with the wings of your protection!'. (Wisecrafting certainly uses ceremony and ritual when appropriate, but can be, and often is, worked anywhere, anytime. Wisecraft draws energy upwards, from the earth. Ceremonial magic tends to draw energy down, from the sky. Ideally they balance each other, and I use both, depending on circumstance.)

MIXING AND MATCHING

Something else to bear in mind is that there may well be more than one planetary influence needed in your work. A creativity charm, for instance, may well fall under abundance (Jupiter), communication (Mercury), and inspiration (Neptune). If you're drawing on the unconscious, you'll also need to add the influence of Pluto. The more complicated the need, the more complicated the spell or charm. This is where the border between 'kitchen witchcraft' and ceremonial magic starts to blur.

Having said that, there's a great deal in favour of keeping it simple. Things are less likely to go wrong, for one thing. And, once again, intention is all. That, and the passionate desire to achieve your aim. Without intense feeling, your spells will remain simply words; your charms will be uncharged bundles of this and that. You won't come to any harm, certainly. But you won't begin to effect change either.

PLANETARY CORRESPONDENCES

The planets of course are named after Roman deities: Mercury, Venus, Mars, Jupiter, Saturn, Uranus, Neptune and Pluto. Each is deemed to have its particular quality or area of influence.

- **Mercury** (Hermes), the Messenger, governs matters of communication and commerce. Plants 'under the influence' of Mercury are those with a sharp, aromatic or clarifying fragrance-lavender, cassia, tea and coffee (and you wondered why you needed that first cup in the morning!), the citruses (lemon, lime, grapefruit). The metal, not surprisingly, is mercury. Any spell is informed by Mercury (it's a verbal or written communication). And most, if not all, charms will benefit from some Mercurial influence, since clear communication is likely to be at least an element in successful completion. The colours associated with Mercury are clear yellow and orange.

- **Venus** (Aphrodite) governs affairs of the heart and matters of comfort, luxury and charm. For example, wearing soft and flowing fabrics, or using satin sheets is very

Aphrodisian. Her association is with sweet-smelling flowers: roses, jasmine, violets, honeysuckle, freesia. Because Aphrodite's myth says that she was born of the sea-foam, seaweeds can also be included in charms, or in cooking! Interestingly, seaweeds are rich in iodine, essential to the health of the endocrine system, which affects hormonal balance. So maybe seaweed soup and sushi are unrecognised aphrodisiacs! Her metal is copper, and her colour is emerald green.

- The energy of **Mars** (Ares) is protective, and also useful in charms or talismans for physical vitality. Sportsmen—footballers, for example—are all under the influence of Mars. Not surprisingly, hot and fiery plants are governed by Mars: chili, nettles and thistles, mustard, garlic, ginger, pepper. As in cooking, it's better to use sparingly—it's possible to OD on Martian energy! Tobacco is also attributed to Mars. His metal is iron, and his colour is clear red.

- **Jupiter** (Zeus) governs abundance and expansiveness. The plant most associated with him is the oak—a tree common enough in southern parts of Australia. (Oak is also the most sacred tree in Druidic tradition). If I'm passing an oak tree I usually take the opportunity to pluck a few leaves—but remember to pay the rent by leaving at least a small coin at the foot of the tree. Silver or golden acorns were worn by noble Roman youths as a protective amulet. You can wear the real thing, or carry an acorn in your pocket to put you in touch with Jupiterian abundance. Other plants are asparagus, hyssop and moneywort. Jupiter's metal is tin, and his colour is royal blue.

- **Saturn** deals with necessary limits (especially those imposed by the laws of karma), the imposition of form and shape, and with inheritance. His tree is the yew, common in English churchyards and the source of the long bow. Many of the plants associated with this planet are poisonous (deadly nightshade, hemlock, monks' bane) or unobtainable. Myrrh is probably the easiest to find and safest to use. It is also used in incense, and a tincture of myrrh can be used externally for the relief of arthritis. Poppies are also associated with Saturn. His metal is lead, and his colour is black.

- **Uranus** governs the auric field and the nervous system. If you are working to help someone suffering depression or nervous agitation, this is the appropriate planetary influence. Allspice, cinnamon, clove and nutmeg are all governed by Uranus. As one of the 'newer' planets (along with Neptune and Pluto) there is no metal traditionally associated with the planet, but in Greek myth he is one of the Titans, so the associated metal might well be titanium. There is no traditional colour association, but violet or the interwoven rainbow seems appropriate.

- **Neptune** (Poseidon), the sea-god, governs the emotional tides and enhances artistic creativity, especially where this involves new ways of seeing—'en-visioning'. Deep-sea plants and animals (whales, dolphins) fall under his influence, as does the lotus and mescal. His colour is sea-green. I would attribute his metal as electrum, an alloy of gold, silver and platinum with Atlantean associations.

- **Pluto** (Hades) is the Lord of the Underworld, the realm of buried treasure and hidden riches, especially the riches of the unconscious, individual and collective. His plants are damiana, eucalyptus, musk, rye, wheat and oats. His colour is dark grey and his metal is uranium.

The other two major influences, not strictly planetary though always included in tables of correspondences, are those of the moon and the sun.

- The **Moon** influences emotions, dreams and intuitive and imaginative insights, so plants and gemstones under the influence of the moon would be useful in charms to enhance creativity. These include all white flowers, but especially the lily and the white lotus, and plants associated with the sea or with water (because of the Moon's influence on the tides): cucumber, watercress, willow. Her colour and metal is silver. Her gem of course is the moonstone.

- The **Sun** brings into the clarity of daylight the dreams and insights given by the astral world of the Moon. In Greek myth they are the twin deities, Artemis and Apollo. Between them, they balance the outer and the inner worlds. Sunflower and marigold, frankincense, bay laurel, rosemary and olive, are all governed by the Sun. So too is the less common eyebright, specific for treating problems of clear vision—you see how herbal medicine and magical herbalism merge! The Sun's metal is gold (but brass is considered an acceptable substitute), as is his colour.

ELEMENTAL CORRESPONDENCES

Celtic wisecrafters use the Four Elements of Earth, Water, Fire and Air, with the fifth element of Spirit, as the basis of their spells and charms. These five are the five points of the pentacle, with the point uppermost representing Spirit which reconciles and harmonises, transforms and transcends earth and air, fire and water.

- **Air** is the element associated with things of the mind, with wit and intellect. Its time is dawn and its season is Spring, the time of fresh starts and new beginnings. Its totems are the birds, especially the hawk and the eagle, who see far and attain the overview of a situation. A bird's feather added to your charm will represent the element of air. Its places are the high and windy places of the planet such as mountain tops, cliff edges. Its god-forms are Myrddin (Merlin), God of high places, and Sarn Elen, Keeper of the Ways (though some place Epona, Horse-Goddess, here). Its colours are the colours of dawn, especially clear yellow, but also very pale blue. In Celtic wisecraft it is placed at the eastern quarter of the circle, and its magical tool is the spear. Feathers may represent the element of air in charms or on your altar. The planetary correspondence is with Mercury.

- **Fire's** time is noon and its season is Summer, when the Sun is in his power. Its qualities are courage, passion and the directed will, the coming to maturity of purpose. Its totems are the stag (for his courage), the lion and the dragon. Its place is the heart of fire, whether on hearth or in smith's forge, candle-flame or bonfire. Its godforms are Lugh Manyskilled and Bride (Brigid/Brigantia), teacher of smiths and poets and healers. Its colour is deep red. In Celtic wisecraft it is placed at the southern quarter of the circle, and its magical tool is the sword. Use something flame-coloured (such as red felt cut into a flame shape) in charm-making, and put a lit candle on your altar. The planetary correspondence is with Mars.

- **Water** is the element associated with the emotions, with the ebb and flow of things, with the power to change. Its time is sunset and moonrise, the place between waking and sleeping, the land of dreams. Its season is Autumn. Its totems are the creatures of the deep, whale and dolphin, and the Salmon of Wisdom—but it is the wisdom of the heart, not the head. Its place is in the mighty oceans and the still pools of healing and contemplation; its song is the sound of a stream over pebbles, or rain on a tin roof. Its godforms are Mananaan Sea-Lord, who guides the glass boat over the sunset sea to the Isles of the Blessed; and Morgan, whose name means 'from the sea', mistress of the magic of change—though some would place Rhiannon of the singing birds here. Its colour is blue or silver. In Celtic wisecraft it is placed at the western quarter of the circle, and its magical tool is the cup. Shells may represent the element of water in charm-making or on your altar. The planetary correspondence is with Venus and the Moon.

- **Earth** represents endurance, steadfastness and the rule of law. Its time is midnight and its season is Winter. Its totems are bear and wolf and badger. Earth's place, like theirs, is in den and cave, especially the crystal cave of initiation. Its godforms are Cernunnos, Lord of Animals, Dancer to the Goddess; and Ceridwen, Lady of the Cauldron of renewal and rebirth. Its colour is deep green. In Celtic wisecraft it is placed at the northern quarter of the circle, the place of mystery, and its magical tool is the round shield inscribed with the pentagram. Salt, rock crystal or a pebble may represent the element of earth in charm-making or on your altar. The planetary correspondence depends on the aspect: Jupiter, Venus and Pluto all play their part.

- **Spirit**, the fifth element, is everywhere and nowhere, between the worlds and in all the worlds, but we place it at the centre of the circle, the still hub of the turning wheel, the heart of being and becoming. It is the heart of music and the heart of silence. It needs neither godform nor symbol: 'For lo, if you do not find me within yourself, you will never find me elsewhere. For I am the beginning and the ending, and I am that which is attained at the end of all desire.'

COLLECTING THE MAKINGS AND PAYING THE RENT

Celtic wisecraft tends to favour the use of found or personally gathered objects. A feather, a shell, a water-smoothed pebble all have their own natural magic. Hawthorn or oak leaves or rosemary you have gathered and dried yourself will contain more of your energy (and less of other people's) and therefore be better fitted to hold your will and intent.

Herbs can be tied in bunches and hung up to dry in your kitchen, or any warm, airy space. An airing cupboard is ideal, if you have one. Above the fridge, where the motor keeps the air warm and circulating, is also good. You can put a paper bag over the leaves and tie the bag loosely around the stalks before hanging the bunch up. This keeps the leaves free of dust and cooking grease. Techno-witches have been known to use the microwave to dry herbs fast!

It is not difficult to gather and dry your own rose petals, jasmine, freesia or whatever. If your partner or family is looking askance at your new interests, you can always tell them you're drying the flowers for potpourri—which, in a sense, you are. And in fact a potpourri made with magical intent (whether to bring peace, happiness or protection to a house or room) is a very powerful charm.

Flower petals can be dried quite easily by putting them into a woven cane basket (flat rather than deep, because too much depth puts the petals at risk of going mouldy) with a couple of sheets of kitchen towel in the bottom. Give it a good shake every day or two to move the petals around, and when they're quite dry, store in a plastic bag. Red petals especially will keep a good colour.

Of course you can buy dried rose petals in craft shops, and if you want to make a love charm before you can dry your own, go ahead. But they won't have the oomph of petals gathered from your own (or a friend's) garden with magical intent in mind, and dried with the same focus on intent. You'll just have to add a bit of extra zing and zap to your charm in other ways—remember, nothing is for nothing.

PAYING THE RENT: NOTHING IS FOR NOTHING

Whenever you gather anything from the natural world—flowers, leaves, seeds, feathers, shells—get into the habit of 'paying the rent'. Give thanks to the tree, plant or place which has provided what you need. This can be a simple thank you, a small coin (traditionally silver, but we no longer use real silver in our coinage), or an offering of grain, milk and honey.

When travelling in the country, here or in Britain, I carry muesli—which combines grain, fruit and honey—as a convenient and inconspicuous offering. There have been many kilos of muesli scattered at stone circles, holy wells, dancing grounds, and at the foot of oak trees and eucalypts over the last fifteen years! Such an offering is of course biodegradable, and will feed the ants or the soil. Remember it's an offering in token, not an opportunity to litter. Banana skins, orange peel or your unwanted cheese sandwich are not appropriate!

In Britain the drink offering is either water from one of the holy wells (such as Chalice Well in Glastonbury), or mead. The spirits of the land in Australia have asked us not to use alcohol in an offering, but milk or water are both very acceptable.

If in doubt, ask the spirits of the place what's appropriate. They will tell you—if you wait, and listen.

Back to basics: what you need to make magic

TO MAKE A SPELL YOU WILL NEED:

- **The words** Choose them with care, try to make sure they define your intent as clearly as possible. Give them a cadence or rhythm. They are an *incantation*, they should sing in the mind and the heart. Spend time, thought and energy on this part of the work. As you get more experienced, you may find that this part of the process becomes the work itself—your words have power. You will also find that with experience the whole process of spellcrafting is, if not easy, then less difficult.

- **The tools** Once you have the words as you want them, the spell may be spoken aloud (courtesy of your vocal chords—no other tools required). This is most suitable if the spell is short and to the point, almost like a mantra.

For instance, before leaving your home in the morning, you may want to say ' Circle and protect my home, all within it and I myself, until I come safe home'. If you also add a visualisation, of, say, a large dragon wrapping itself over the roof-line and resting a dragonish chin on the front doorstep, you'll find your sense of security greatly enhanced. And in this case, the more often you perform this mini-ritual, the stronger the protection will get.

The other kind of spell directed at a specific need or circumstance, may be more effective if inscribed, written down in a fair (and careful) copy.

INSCRIBING A SPELL

You may want to do this in a prepared and cleansed ritual space. At the least, the area should be clean, and you should light a candle to signal the seriousness of your intent. The colour of the candle should be chosen to harmonise with the nature of the spell (see Chapter Three). If this is serious work (and what isn't?) check the phase of the moon—you may need to modify your spell accordingly (refer to Chapter Eight for more information).

To inscribe your spell, tradition calls for parchment—by which they mean vellum. It was originally made from calfskin—I won't go into gruesome detail! True vellum parchment is still obtainable (with some difficulty), but it needs to be specially prepared before it can be written on. It is simpler to get parchment-style paper. Art shops and some good stationers will have this; it's sometimes called calligraphy paper. The alternative is to use coloured paper—choose the colour in accordance with the type of spell.

Then you'll need pen and ink.

I really don't recommend running spells off on your computer, even if you do have Celtic or American Uncial typefaces. Old-fashioned of me, I know. I'm also old-fashioned enough to dislike felt-tip and ballpoint pens for the actual making (inscribing) of the spell, though they're acceptable when you're working on the rough drafts.

On the other hand, making your own ink seems a touch labour-intensive, and it's so difficult to get oak galls and lampblack nowadays! Goose quills look great but are tricky to keep in working order. The point wears down quickly—that's what a pen-knife was originally intended for, to sharpen your pen! And quills do tend to spatter and blob.

Fountain pens (or calligraphy pens) and a range of coloured inks will cover most contingencies. The coloured inks? Red, green, blue and violet should cover most eventualities. Gold and silver as well, if you like—but you can't generally use these in a fountain pen, as they clog the works.

Once your spell is inscribed, what then? Fold it to a convenient size and carry it next to your skin for a night and a day (sunset to sunset). After sunset, read it aloud (with energy and emotion) and then burn it in the flame of the candle you lit to inscribe it. This releases the spell to do its work.

You may choose to keep any residual ash or scraps of paper in a *spellbox*.

TO MAKE A CHARM YOU WILL NEED:

- **The container** A circle of new cloth or leather. Cord, thread or wool (red is always a good colour—remember, it's the colour associated with fire, courage and will). White is also good, because it contains all colours. If you're using leather, you may want to make small holes around the edge to take a drawstring. Bear in mind that if you choose leather, you are also involving the energy of the God who is Lord of the Hunt in Celtic wisecraft. This may or may not be appropriate, depending on the nature of the charm.

- **The contained** Herbs, spices, found objects (shells, stones, feathers) chosen according to correspondence or element. These are put in the centre of the cloth, the edges drawn together, and the cord tied (like a Christmas pudding) to keep all in place. If you've done a kitchen-sink charm (everything in it but . . . !) make sure your cloth is large enough to hold the goodies. If the end result is the size of a football, perhaps you need to re-think the focus of the charm.

  My charms usually include sugar to sweeten the outcome, salt for savour (and to ground the charm), a pigeon's feather to speed the energy on its way (and bring it home again), and sesame (seeds) to open doors (as it did for Aladdin!).

- **The charge** Once your charm is assembled, you need to *charge* or *empower* it. There are several ways of doing this. Holding it in your hands and directing energy into it (for example, by kneading it) is one method. You can also chant at the same time. Since most charms are intended to effect change, the chant 'She changes everything She touches, and everything She touches, changes' may well be effective—especially if this is done at full moon, under the light of a full moon. For a protective charm, try the Goddess chant 'Isis, Astarte, Diana, Hecate, Demeter, Kali, Inanna' (available on a tape, *From the Goddess*, by Robert Glass).

Other methods: carry the charm on your person for a night and a day (sunset to sunset) before putting it in the appropriate place. Set up a formal circle and charge or bless the charm by holding it over the candle flame dedicated to each element. Or, more simply:

ELEMENTAL BLESSING OF A CHARM

✦ Blow on the charm (air), and say '*Powers of Air, bless and inform this charm*'.

✦ Hold it over a candle flame (fire), and say: '*Powers of Fire, bless and enliven this charm*'.

✦ Sprinkle it with water, and say: '*Powers of Water, bless and empower this charm*'.

✦ Touch it to earth or a pentagram or sprinkle it with salt (earth) and say: '*Powers of Earth, bless and make fruitful this charm*'. Putting salt in the charm itself helps ground the work—salt represents the element of earth in my tradition.

✦ Hold the charm above your head in both hands, and say '*Power of Spirit, Reconciler, bless this charm and its maker. For the good of all and according to the free will of all this work is done. So be it.*'

◎ **Placing the charm** It stands to reason that a house-protection charm should be pinned up over the door, a love charm is carried on your person, a car-protection charm hangs in the car or is hidden under the driver's seat, and so on. I've already said that I have an abundance charm next to my computer. My lawyer keeps his in his office desk.

- **What to do when it's done its work** At the end of a year and a day, or sooner if you feel that the charm has done its work, the charm should be disassembled and the contents returned to the elements—herbs scattered on the ground, stones or other objects buried as an offering to the Mother. Dispose also of the cloth in which the charm was tied. Give thanks for the successful completion of the work.

  There are a couple of reasons for this. First, nothing is forever. You have bound certain objects and energies to a particular work. If the work is successfully completed, it will not be harmed by dispersal of the charm. And you no longer need the support the charm provided.

  If, on the other hand, the charm was not successful, you need to ask yourself why (did you shoot yourself in the foot? See 'Acting in Accordance', above). With this insight you can make a new and hopefully better charm. Remember, She changes everything She touches, and everything She touches changes. Are you keeping yourself open to change?

TO MAKE AN AMULET

Unless you use Beyerl's method from *The Master Book of Herbalism* (a leather bag which holds herbs and symbolic objects on a permanent basis), making your own amulet may demand skills outside your capacity. You could of course take jewellery and silversmithing classes—or you may be fortunate enough to have already acquired these skills.

For most of us, it's more a case of looking for the appropriate or significant symbol and then dedicating it to its purpose by any of the methods outlined above. If your chosen amulet is linked to a particular form or face of the Goddess or the God, you will probably choose to ask their help or protection in this. It can be done as simply or elaborately as you like.

The new moon is always a good time to charge and dedicate an amulet, since starting to wear one is a sign that you wish to start a new phase of your life.

If you just can't find the right amulet, or you've seen a symbol in a dream and want to reproduce it, consider having it made. There are silversmiths around who have an understanding of, or at least sympathy for, magic. Ask your local esoteric bookshop who they get their jewellery from, or see Suppliers and Resources at the end of this book. Woodcarving or engraving is another possibility.

TO MAKE A TALISMAN

See my remarks above on the complexity of this operation. But if you decide to do this, you'll need parchment, pen, ink, and (traditionally) black silk to wrap and then sew it into. Talismans are usually empowered by reference to the archangel(s) in whose name they were made, or by drawing down power from the Most High.

Talismans customarily use a variety of sigils (symbols) and/or magical alphabets to direct the maker's intent.

The sigils are based on a system of magical squares (kameas) and are linked to the planets and the planetary intelligences (angels or archangels, seraphim, cherubim ...). A good book on talismanic magic will give more than enough examples.

The alphabets include: Hebrew, Enochian, Egyptian (hieroglyphs), Chaldean, Theban, Angelic, Malachim, Runic (Germanic, Scandinavian, Anglo-Saxon), and Ogham (Druidic). Runic is used by followers of the Northern tradition (Asatru, Norse) and Ogham by diligent Druids. The rest are used mainly by ceremonial magicians.

The advantage of the alphabets is the amount of concentration required to make sense of any of them, and then draw them with absolute correctness and precision. Personally, I find life is so much simpler if I use English! Then all concerned are clear as to my aim and intent.

But if you want to try your hand at talismanic magic, you can use the astrological symbol instead of the sigil for the energy you want to draw down. And you can use purely personal symbolism.

Suppose you're looking for the perfect house to buy or rent. You can draw your ideal house, or its floor-plan. Enclose it in a square (for manifestation on the physical plane) inside a double circle (for completion and protection). Between the inner and outer rings write your spell, for instance 'the perfect house for me and mine'. In the four spaces between the square and the circle, inscribe the appropriate astrological symbols for the influences you want to draw on.

For a house-finding talisman these would probably be Jupiter (for abundance of food, drink and good company, and money to pay the rent or mortgage), Mercury (because this is a commercial transaction) and Venus (for that touch of luxury that every home needs). Personalise the talisman by using as the fourth symbol the Zodiac sign appropriate to your birthday. Fold it in four and charge (empower) it. Rather than calling on the archangels, you can use the Elemental Blessing given above. Wrap and/or sew the talisman in green silk and carry it next to your skin to further empower it.

Talismans are normally carried on the person or (for money talismans) in the wallet. They are much more common in ceremonial magic than in wisecraft, but a wisecrafted talisman is a very effective piece of long-term magic. Note 'long-term'—my experience of talismans is that they can take months, sometimes years, to achieve a result.

In summary,

- Decide the form: spell, charm, amulet, or talisman?

- Decide on the appropriate correspondence(s) or element.
- Assemble the doings.
- Chant the spell, charge the charm.
- Act in accordance.

And remember the four rules of all magical work:

- Words carry energy: words are power
- Do harm to none
- Define your terms!
- There are no setbacks, only unrealised opportunities.

Chapter Two

getting started: so what do i do now?

'A trained magician can work magic in a desert or a supermarket with no tools other than hands, heart, mind and will.'

Dolores Ashcroft-Nowicki

Many books on magic go into great detail on the equipment deemed necessary to work magic: altar, assorted incenses, candles in various colours, pentacle (five-pointed star enclosed in a circle), chalice (a stemmed goblet), athame (black-handled ritual short blade), boline (white-handled knife), wand, cords, Book of Shadows . . . the list goes on and on.

So how much of this do you actually need?

That's rather a 'how long is a piece of string?' kind of question. You need as much as you need to convince yourself that you can make effective magic. Minimalist witches—kitchen witches—use what happens to be on hand. Common kitchen herbs and spices, flowers from the garden, shells and seaweed gathered the last time you walked along the beach—simple ingredients. I have acquired, over the years, all the fixtures and fittings (and then some!) of the Compleat Magico. However, I now only rarely feel the need to use them. Magic is in the head, the heart and the will—not in objects, however beautiful.

Ritual tools, like so much else in magic, help focus the attention and the will. There is no *intrinsic* magic in, say, a wand or a chalice. Over a period of time and with constant use, however, a magical tool builds up a chain of associations—Rupert Sheldrake uses the term 'morphic resonance'—which is triggered every time the tool is used, and which contacts the archetype of that particular kind of power or force.

These tools can and do develop a zap potential which is very obvious to the sensitive. They also become strongly identified with their owner/user; in a sense, they become attuned to one person's vibratory rate. Handling by someone else can, it is believed, disturb this subtle connection. This is one reason why you should NEVER handle someone else's magical equipment unless specifically invited to do so.

In group work, the ritual preparation of the working area helps those present to set aside mundane cares and thoughts, and to move wholly into sacred space, the space 'between the worlds' where magic is made. If you are working solo, preparation of yourself and your working space is important because that helps your transition from the everyday concerns of your life. But if you are starting out and working on your own, you can get by with very little in the way of magical tools.

It's better to start off simply and acquire what you need when you really need it. You don't have to send off for somebody's Complete Priestess Kit ('all you need to become your own priestess . . . assembled by an authentic Wiccan High Priestess'). You are already your own priestess (or priest, as the case may be) and need no-one else's blessing save that of the Goddess or God in whose name you work.

There are, however, some items it is useful to have on hand

for spellcrafting and charm-making, though a lot of the ingredients for charms will be gathered as you need them.

Under general equipment (like plates, bowls and cups in your kitchen) I would suggest you acquire:

Equipment for spellcrafting and talisman-making

- Good quality paper, such as Conqueror Parchment, on which to inscribe the spell or talisman, once formulated.

- Ink with which to inscribe it—you can use any colour, including black. But it can add oomph if you choose a colour ink appropriate to the spell or talisman. All the inks below are obtainable from a good pen shop or stationer's—though if you don't live in a capital city, you may need to place a special order.
  - Red for protection—the colour of Mars. (But royal blue is a good colour to use for defence against psychic attack, because of its association with the Goddess Isis.)
  - Midnight blue (navy) for abundance—the colour of Jupiter.
  - Green for fertility and healing, and for some love spells (associated with Venus).
  - Violet for spiritual issues.
  - Gold ink for talismans of the Sun, silver for talismans of the Moon.
  - Brown or sepia for old-fashioned values!

- A pen to do the inscribing—calligraphy pens are good, but don't use them for gold and silver inks as they will clog.

Equipment for charm-making

- A selection of felt squares (or pure cotton, wool or linen) in various colours:
  - White—contains all colours, so all-purpose
  - The Quarter colours (the colours associated in my tradition with Air, Fire, Water and Earth—other traditions use other colour attributions):
    - yellow for matters of intellect and communication (Air)
    - red for matters requiring courage and passion (Fire)
    - blue for matters of emotion, change and flow (Water)
    - green for fertility, groundedness and endurance (Earth)
    - white, violet or purple for affairs of love and affection—not love-as-lust (Spirit).

- The necessary herbs, spices, tumbled stones, symbolic items (e.g. a silver key of the kind bought for charm bracelets, to open doors—useful for a job-getting charm). You'll normally buy or acquire these for a specific charm, but you may want to have the following to hand (some perhaps grown and dried by you):
  - Rose petals or rosebuds—for love charms, or for charms requiring, well, charm!
  - Sandalwood—bark, powder, chips or essential oil—for protection from negativity, including your own.
  - Sesame seed—for opening doors ('Open, sesame!' as Ali Baba said to open the cave full of treasure).
  - Small dried chili peppers (birdseye chilis)—for protection charms.
  - Lavender—for protection, purification and the powers of mind.
  - Bird feathers—to add wings to the charm.

- Your kitchen will already have
  - sugar (to sweeten the outcome)
  - salt (for savour and to ground, or earth, the charm).
- Ribbon, silk thread (embroidery thread) or wool to tie or sew up the charm once its components are assembled.

Do I need an altar?

You need a place to work magic. Wherever you work magic becomes, for that time, an altar. Great-Granny Smith used her kitchen table (if she had one), a fallen tree or that nice flat rock over by the spring.

You can practise meditation or do the Fountain exercise (see Chapter Six) in a candle-lit bathroom, choosing aromatherapy oils instead of incense. For that time, the bathroom becomes sacred space.

You can clear your dressing table of all the lotions and potions you own but never use, and use that as an altar. All it takes is a candle and a few flowers in a pretty vase.

TO SET UP AN ALTAR OF THE ELEMENTS

You don't need to have 'witchy' implements (pentacle, cup, wand and blade) to set up an altar to work earthmagic. You can just as effectively mark the Quarters and ask the presence of the elemental powers by using the appropriate natural things, found rather than bought. So, on the top of your altar-box, put a cloth (a silk scarf in rainbow colours will work beautifully) and then arrange, in a way pleasing to you:

✦ For the **element of Air:**

- feathers-pigeon feathers float around most city streets;
- perfumed flowers from your garden (rose, jasmine, lavender).

✦ For the **element of Fire:**

- a candle flame;
- a red chili pepper.

✦ For the **element of Water:**

- a glass of water (or wine)—a crystal wineglass looks good;
- a seashell-a cowrie (always a female symbol—look at its in-folded shape!) or scallop shell (symbol of pilgrimage—and the concave shape means it can also hold a little water).

✦ For the **element of Earth:**

- a tumbled stone—one of the agates, such as chalcedony;
- rock salt in a terracotta dish;
- a small bundle of herbs from your garden—thyme is good.

✦ For the **element of Spirit:**

- a clear quartz crystal or a piece of amethyst.

Of course, you can have all these things artistically arranged on a table or mantelpiece in your living room, and nobody (except a fellow earthmagician) will be any the wiser!

HOUSE ALTARS

These can also look like a simple arrangement of pleasing objects. You may have a shelf at home or in your office which will take, for example, a piece of rose quartz, a small statue of Kuan Yin (Chinese Goddess of Compassion), and a flower in a vase. Focusing on this, however briefly, during a busy day will bring tranquillity into your life for a few moments. Spells to do with a harmonious workplace can be placed under the statue to be charged, as can healing spells. Charms will tuck inconspicuously alongside.

If you're lucky, you can be completely open about your interests. An altar to Aphrodite in the bedroom, another to Athena (Greek goddess of wisdom) in the office, Mnemosyne (her name means Memory and she's the mother of the Muses) alongside the computer, a collection of owls (sacred to Athena) in the living room, Celts in the kitchen, Egyptians in the hall . . .

If you're very, very lucky, you can set aside a room to be used solely for meditation and magic—temple space. But if you can't, don't fret. And don't put off working because you haven't got all the fixtures and fittings!

Whatever you can do, or dream you can, begin it.
Boldness has genius, magic and power in it.
Begin it now!
J.W. Von Goethe

After a while, you may cease to care if people know about your interests. But if your employment depends on your discretion (you're a teacher in a church-run school, for example), then be discreet. A friend who's an engineer describes his weekends away at various magical events as 'attending a conference on alternative forms of energy'. It's usually assumed he's gone to a workshop on windmills or solar power.

Most people hear what they want to hear. You don't need to lie—just choose your words with care. 'An interest in alternative healing' is also a useful phrase, as is 'stress management' for meditation classes.

There really is nothing to prevent you from working magic except that nagging voice of the ego finding reasons why you can't, or shouldn't, or oughtn't.

It's all too easy to let your own needs be swamped by the needs and demands of your job, your children, your partner, your extended family. But remember, when you hesitate to take over a corner of the house or your bedroom, that in the midst of even the busiest, most family-filled life you have the right to take time and space for yourself. If you do not refresh your spirit, you will end by having nothing more to give.

If guilt and self-doubt make it difficult for you to claim time and space for yourself, use the following spell every day to strengthen your resolve.

SPELL TO CLAIM YOUR OWN SPACE

✦ Look at your face in the mirror—first thing in the morning is a good time, before the cares of the day have had time to hit. See yourself as you really are-a garment of the Goddess. Say aloud:

I have the right and the duty to take time and space to refresh my spirit, today and every day. Unless I am refreshed, I cannot continue to give.

I acknowledge the presence of the Goddess in me and know that I can give more fully to those I love if I am myself refreshed and nurtured.

- Smile at your reflection and go about your busy day. Repeat every day until you no longer need the spell.

If privacy is a problem—inquisitive children, nosy flatmates—consider buying or having made a wooden box which can be locked. This is your portable altar and magical storage space. Keep your spellcasting and charm-making materials inside, together with any other magical equipment (candles, altar cloth, symbols of the elements, magical diary, notebook of spells, recipes for charms and a record of their effect).

Preparation of Place: creating sacred space

Sacred space is a particular area set aside for personal and/or magical work.

A place dedicated solely to ritual and magical work—a lodge, covenstead, temple or grove—builds up, over time, an atmosphere that can be like walking into a closed door. This is partly a function of the kind of work done there, and partly the result of a regular reinforcement of the wards. You can find the same atmosphere of concentrated stillness in some old churches.

But most of us have to adapt to available space and circumstance.

The space needs to be big enough to contain you and your altar or designated working area (your desk or dressing table, for example)—although at a pinch it need extend no further than the outer rim of your aura. It is made sacred by being dedicated to your purpose on that occasion. It returns to normal household use (if you do your magical work at home, as most of us do) when you've done what you need to.

Creating sacred space can be as simple or as complicated as you choose. The first thing you need to do is clean your working area. Yes, *clean*. Vacuum, mop or sweep the floor, tidy the vicinity. Dust if necessary. As a wise old witch once said to me, 'Nobody has a soul above housework!'. Making order in this way makes space in your life for magic.

After the working area is physically clean, there are various methods for giving it an astral scrub-and-polish.

- You can *asperge* the area—sprinkle it with a mixture of salt and water using, for example, a sprig of rosemary or basil.

- You can *smudge* the room using the smoke from a bundle of dried herbs tied together so that they smoulder rather than burn. This method is used in both Native American and Koori traditions. It can also be used to cleanse an aura as part of healing work.

- You can *cense* the room using a thurible and a consecration/purification incense.

- After any of these, you can *cast a circle* using an athame (ritual blade) to protect you and contain magical energies until you are ready to send them on their way.

As you can see, this can get quite involved. For simple wise-crafting, I find it's sufficient to light a candle and visualise the light from the flame spreading out to cleanse and consecrate the space. Accompany this with a *spell* such as:

SPELL TO CREATE SACRED SPACE

✦ Light a white or violet candle and say:

Powers above and Powers below
Powers without and Powers within
Circle and protect me
Guide, guard, heal and hallow me
And bring me safe home.

✦ Spend some moments visualising the protective and cleansing power radiating from the candle flame, through you and out into your working area. Then say:

It is done. This space and all within it is cleansed and hallowed. It is done.

You and your space are now ritually prepared to carry out the work you have decided on.

When you have finished your work, thank the Powers. Something like 'I thank you for your presence and your blessing. I thank you for your help in my work. Until we meet again, hail and farewell' is perfectly adequate.

I have been taught that the Powers, mighty as they are, gain benefit from working with humankind. Though at one level it seems more than a touch arrogant, it is appropriate for us to give them our blessing as it is for us to ask their blessing on our work. So when I have asked or named specific powers (for example, Michael Archangel), I speak to them by name and say: 'I give you my thanks and my blessing. Hail, and farewell.'

Some rituals use the formula 'I summon, stir, and call thee

up' and then require you to 'banish' the powers so summoned at the end of the rite. This has always seemed to me to be, at the least, lacking in courtesy. I prefer to invite, asking rather than demanding their help, and then farewell, as one would an honoured guest.

Preparation of Person

You're going out to a social event at which you know you'll meet influential people—people who can put work your way, or ease an important social or business connection. Do you turn up with unwashed hair, shabby clothes, unbrushed teeth? Not if you have any social skills or sense of occasion! At the very least, your person and clothing will be clean and neat. You will probably have gone to at least a little extra trouble to look your best.

When you work magic, you are working with the Powers that have shaped the Universe. Are they less important to you than a business or social contact?

Magic can, at need, be worked naked in a desert or while shopping in your local supermarket. Wisecrafting doesn't demand silken robes and dedicated temple space. But preparation of person and place signals to your inner self that what you are about to do is significant, important. It helps you move into that sacred space within which magic finds fulfilment.

Even if you choose to work skyclad (naked), you should take time to bathe or shower. Use one of the aura cleansing mixtures given in Chapter Six to ensure that you bring nothing untoward into your working space. It will also help you separate yourself from the events of the day, and clear your mind for the work in hand.

TO ROBE OR NOT TO ROBE?

You may choose to make or buy a robe or dress to wear for magical work. If you do, it should be something special, different in style to your everyday clothes. It needn't be black. I most often wear a deep green satin robe with Celtic knotwork on the sleeves. One friend wears a loose Indian cotton dress in shades of violet, another (male and a martial artist) has based his robes on a combination of judo jacket and kimono. (He in fact usually wears black, as do the Ninja.)

Earthmagicians may wear anything from tweeds and wellies (gumboots) to nothing at all, although as a good friend living in the English countryside remarked, 'Any fool who works naked outdoors in this climate deserves to come down with pneumonia!'

But most of us like to play dress-ups as much as the next magico, so (according to taste and budget) the usual working gear in a coven will be:

- a robe (any colour, any style—green is a popular colour). Men are as likely to wear trews and a plaid as a robe;
- an athame (ritual short blade);
- a belt (to hang the athame from);
- jewellery to taste—the preferred metal is silver, sacred to the Goddess;
- bare feet.

If you often work outdoors and are not sure if the area is free of prickles, cowpats and broken glass, you may choose to wear sandals (or something with thin soles, as near to barefoot as practicable). You may also want to invest, for cold weather, in a wood-cloak—usually dark green, brown or black wool, all the better for inconspicuously slipping away into the bush in. (There are old stories about witches being able to disappear when disturbed at their rites. What really happened was that they put on wood-cloaks, pulled up the hoods, and became 'invisible' to observers.)

If you think all this is getting a bit elaborate, take a look at the working garb of a ceremonial magician.

- a robe—in fact, two robes. The Inner Robe of Glory (white) is covered by the Outer Robe of Concealment (usually black);
- the *cingulum*, a cord in the colour of his status or degree within a lodge;
- possibly a tabard (a loose surcoat open at the sides) in the colour appropriate to the ritual or his place in it (e.g. gold for rituals of the Sun and of the sephira *Tiphareth*);
- a cloak (with hood, if his robe doesn't have one);
- temple slippers (worn only within the temple or consecrated area);
- possibly headgear (the nemyss, a kind of folded scarf like those worn by ancient Egyptians or some modern Druids);
- a lamen (magical symbol) over the heart chakra;
- jewellery appropriate to the rite—for example, a copper belt decorated with emeralds for a rite of Venus;
- a magical ring;
- a wand appropriate to the rite or the Quarter being held; and
- possibly a sword.

There are also special robing prayers to accompany the putting on of every garment from slippers to nemyss.

In my tradition, the equivalent is a self-blessing ritual performed after the shower or bath and before robing.

SELF-BLESSING SPELL

✦ You will need a small amount of perfumed oil. You may use an all-purpose meditation oil (frankincense, sandalwood) or add a few drops of jasmine (Goddess) or oakmoss (God) essential oils to a carrier oil such as almond. Anoint each part of the body as it is blessed—a fingertip touch is adequate.

✦ Say:
Bless me, Mother, for I am Thy child.
Blessed be my feet, which have brought me in these ways.
Blessed be my knees, which shall kneel at Thy altar.
Blessed be my sex, which has the power to create life and give joy—
Even as You create life and give joy.
Blessed be my breasts, formed in strength and beauty,
Blessed be my lips, which shall speak the words of power and of love.
I in Thee, and Thou in me, now and always.

Whatever you wear, putting it on (or taking it off, if you work skyclad) acts as a further signal to your inner self that something important is about to happen. Every garment, every small preparatory ritual, helps the wearer to move 'between the worlds'—to that place that is not a place, in a time that is not a time, where all things are coming into being and all things are possible.

Closing down after working magic

If the work has gone particularly well—especially if you've been chanting—you may feel quite 'buzzy' and even a little high or lightheaded. This can be very pleasant, and there's a real temptation to hang in there and enjoy the sensation. You are, however, psychically open, and the slightest disharmony—somebody slamming a door or turning up the TV—can be very disquieting. In addition, your reflexes and physical coordination may be affected. Driving a car in this heightened state is an absolute no-no!

A hot drink and a light snack are the best and simplest way of grounding after work. Some people take the trouble to have a flask of soup and a sandwich ready and waiting. But coffee and a Tim Tam will also do the trick.

If you are working outdoors, or in a place that isn't your own (public hall, motel room) it's a good idea (and sound psychic hygiene) to *do a gather* after you've finished working. This is a practice and technique I learned from Paddy Slade, author of *Diary of a Village Witch*.

GATHERING IN

✦ Stand in the middle of your working area (if in a room) or pace the perimeter of your circle (if outside). Using both hands, gesture in to yourself, as if you were hauling in a rope, or summoning someone to come closer. Continue the action while pacing, or facing each corner of the room in turn, and say:

Gather in, gather in
All that here has been.
Gather in, gather in
That no trace be seen.
No trace to mar the nights and days
Of those that do not share our ways.
Gather in, gather in
All that here has been.

✦ You have wound up any undispersed energy into a bundle between your hands. You may either ground it by touching the floor (or if possible, the earth), or draw it into yourself by placing your hands on your solar plexus. If this makes you feel lightheaded (which it may if you are working indoors), go outside at once and hug the nearest tree!

I hope that I am beginning to convince you that natural magic is, well, completely natural. As practised by our foremothers, it requires only the simplest of tools and ingredients. Why, then, do so many books on magic say that you absolutely must have this, that or the other item for your spell to scintillate or your charm to be truly captivating?

Books on witchcraft sometimes give a checklist of essential equipment. For example:

- athame (ritual knife, black-handled)—to cast the circle;
- boline (white-handled knife)—to cut herbs;
- wand;
- chalice;

- pentacle;
- cord to draw the circle (traditionally it has a nine-foot diameter—forget metrics!);
- scourge;
- Book of Shadows;
- assorted candles;
- thurible and incenses.

Believe me, you can make perfectly good magic without any of these. Each has its use and function, but it's so easy to get caught up in having the right equipment (and some of these things are quite difficult to find) that you forget your original purpose—to make magic happen in your life.

The one ritual tool I suggest you take time and trouble to acquire is the *athame* (pronunciation varies—a-thay-me, a-thar-me, but either way it is stressed on the second syllable).

The blade is a symbol of your will, forged in the fire of your courage. It is used to focus and direct energy, to mark out and claim sacred space. I think it's a particularly important magical tool for women, because it represents a kind of power that we are nervous about claiming for our own.

Some people are reluctant to handle blades, even to have a sharp knife in their kitchen—though a sharp blade is in fact safer to use than a blunt one. One friend, when she first started out in magic, chose to use a wooden blade until she had come into her power sufficiently to be comfortable with steel.

Look for a knife to suit your hand (most women find a full-sized Bowie a bit tiring in the long term). Traditionally the athame has a blade which is capable of being sharpened on both sides (like a commando knife), A leaf-blade or a stiletto are also acceptable. All look like miniature swords, one of the oldest symbols of power.

You may choose to leave it unsharpened, as it's not supposed to be used to cut anything. I can't myself see the point in owning a blunt knife, but then I like blades and always have.

The idea behind the shape of the blade (apart from making clear its similarity to a sword) is that it's easier to direct power in a straight line, and the curvy bits will tend to deflect the line. I'm not sure I agree with that—look at the curling wave just before it crashes down, or the blade of the Malay *kris*, which was believed to be so magical that certain blades could kill without physical contact.

So if you find a blade that isn't the 'required' shape but still comes easily to your hand, use it. Great-Granny Smith probably only had one knife (they were valuable articles in her day) and used it for everything from skinning rabbits to cutting herbs.

Because of its symbolism, it's generally better to start off with a new blade. You are beginning a new phase of your life, and your will to change and grow begins afresh from this point. You also won't have to work as hard to cleanse it of any past associations as you would with a knife bought, for example, in an antique shop.

If however, the blade you find (or that finds you) is an old one, you will need to cleanse it before using it in magic. In fact, it's a good idea to cleanse any blade, even a 'new' one, before using it—it will have been handled by who-knows-who before it comes to you. But it doesn't have to be engraved with mystic runes or blessed and charged by Ipsissimus, Magus or even a Wiccan High Priestess. Use the following:

ELEMENTAL SPELL TO CLEANSE AND BLESS A BLADE

✦ Give the knife a good wash and polish before you start, and use a moisture-excluding compound like WD40 to oil it. Then:

✦ Take the blade between both hands and blow along its length, saying: *Powers of Air, cleanse and bless this blade and make it fit for my purpose.*

✦ Pass the blade through the flame of a candle and say: *Powers of Fire, cleanse and bless this blade and make it fit for my purpose.*

✦ Hold the blade under running water, so that the water runs from hilt to blade point, and say: *Powers of Water, cleanse and bless this blade and make it fit for my purpose.*

✦ Touch the blade to the earth or a dish of salt, and say: *Powers of Earth, cleanse and bless this blade and make it fit for my purpose.*

✦ Hold the blade above your head, and say: *Power of Spirit, Power of the Goddess Without and the Goddess Within, cleanse and bless this blade and make it fit for my purpose. Charge and empower it as you charge and empower me, that it may always be a symbol of my magical Will and my true purpose. So I will, and it is so.* (A man may wish to use the phrase '*Power of the God Without and the God Within*', if this seems appropriate.)

✦ If this can be performed at the time of the full moon and in the open air, so much the better. The light of the moon shining along the blade will reinforce the spell as nothing else can.

✦ Make sure the blade is clean and dry before wrapping it in silk and storing it safely until the next time you need to use it.

If you are offered a blade as a gift, follow your instincts as to whether you should accept it. Remember its symbolism. Those who give power can also take it back. Should you decide to accept the gift, you must give the giver a coin in payment. Not to do so, according to folklore, will cut the friendship. I am told by a friend who is a smith that the coin—the 'payment'—cuts the bond between the blade and its maker (or giver) and frees it to its new service. It also frees the maker of responsibility for how the blade is subsequently used.

Other magical tools derive their significance from the quarter at which they stand, and can be used accordingly, but you don't actually *need* them to empower the spell or charm.

- The wand (originally perhaps an arrow or spear) represents the power of Air, the power of mind and clear thought. Spells, which are thought out and then spoken, are by their very nature all under the influence of Air. They can be wound around a wand to give them extra oomph. Charms to do with clear thought and communication can be charged using a wand.

- The chalice represents the power of water, the power of emotion and the power to change. Tradition says that (unlike the athame) the chalice should be a gift rather than a purchase. Love-spells and charms can be placed in the chalice when you charge them. The chalice is used in the ritual of Drinking Down the Moon, a self-empowerment ritual to draw Goddess-power into the drinker.

- The pentacle (a disc or platter on which the pentagram is painted, carved or engraved) represents the power of Earth, of groundedness, stability and endurance. Spells and charms can be *grounded* (their purpose helped into manifestation in the real world) by being placed on the pentacle, or left there overnight at a full moon.

But always remember, ultimately the four tools of magic are not wand, athame, cup and pentacle but wit, will, desire and endurance.

The four tools of magic: wit, will, desire, endurance

Of the other 'necessary' tools, the Book of Shadows gets a lot of attention. In some traditions, during your apprenticeship you hand-copy a version of the rituals worked by your particular group or coven into your own Book of Shadows. There's a great deal of mystique surrounding the original Book from which all copies are supposedly derived. Some groups do the 'our Book of Shadows is more authentic than your Book of Shadows' number.

In fact, most of these rituals derive from Gerald Gardner's rewriting of the fragments of lore he had from his New Forest coven. The result was much influenced by Gardner's knowledge of Freemasonry and by Doreen Valiente's skill as a ritual poet—it's generally acknowledged now that the beautiful Charge of the Goddess is her work. (Gerald Gardner gave his name to Gardnerian Wicca and Valiente was his High Priestess. It is thought by some that Valiente wrote, or at least co-wrote, the Gardnerian Book of Shadows.) These rituals are fine, and at times very beautiful, but they're not ancient—unless you consider circa 1950 ancient.

Our Great-Granny Smith may well have been unable to read or write. She relied instead on a trained memory and a lifetime of experience of what really worked. She also devised her rituals and spells as she needed them. They were unlikely to be the same two times running, because the circumstance, or the material to hand, was likely to be different.

It is however useful, in these days of universal literacy and poor memory, to keep a record of spells, charms and their outcome. Call it your Book of Shadows if you like. It's also useful to keep a magical diary and a dream journal. It can be interesting to look back and see where you started from.

But you need to have a life, and there are only so many hours in a day. I have a fridge magnet that says 'Life happens while you're busy making other plans'. Magic can become a preoccupation, even an obsession. Keep all this in perspective.

Group work or solitary magic?

There's an old saying, 'You cannot be a witch alone'. This is arrant nonsense. You can, and when you're starting out, you probably should, work alone. That way, you have a better chance of finding out what works for you, rather than simply following your leader. You have time to build your own strength, work out your ethical position on, say, love spells and charms, or healing work.

If you work in a group, the probability is that you will be the newest member. The others will be, or seem to be, more confident, better informed, more capable. In such a situation it's very easy for your judgement to be swayed by 'we've always done it this way', even when your inner alarm bells are ringing.

A good few years ago now, I was invited to meet, at a friend's house, a woman with a considerable reputation as a magico. We met, we chatted, we got on well. Then she said that she'd been asked to do some empowerment work for a close friend who was about to give a paper at a conference on food irradiation. He was presenting the case against, and the food industry had some pretty heavy guns lined up to argue the case in favour.

The magico decided that the way to go was to focus on the food industry representatives and plant in their minds uncertainty and doubt as to the rightness of their position. So far, so good. But the way she opted to do this was by setting up a chant: 'uncertainty and doubt . . . uncertainty and doubt . . .' Alarm bells started to ring, but she was much more experienced in this sort of thing than I was. I assumed she knew what she was doing. So we chanted.

Within a couple of weeks the man who'd asked for help had telephoned the magico to say that he'd decided their relationship was over. Since until then he'd been saying she was the love of his life, this was a great and painful blow to her.

The 'uncertainty and doubt' had certainly been projected, but it had not found the intended target. In hindsight, the magico had presumably been thinking about her friend (whose face she knew) rather than about the faceless food industry reps. And she'd chosen the wrong chant for the work she'd been asked to do. Something like 'Give (name) power and persuasion', with 'power and persuasion' as the ascending chant, would have been more appropriate. Of course, the relationship might have collapsed anyway. But the timing was, well, interesting. It was a salutary lesson in being careful what you ask for.

There are undoubtedly advantages to working in or with a group. For one thing, you're probably more likely to work regularly. Most covens or circles will work at full moon and dark moon, as well as at the Eight Festivals (see Chapter Eight). This may require more commitment than you were ever prepared to give Christianity! You'll be meeting at least once a fortnight, and (if there's a major festival) sometimes weekly. So you're actually likely to get more practice than you would as a solitary.

It's also a matter of observation that even two people working together raise more energy than the two working solo. There seems to be an exponential increase in available magical energy—the whole is decidedly greater than the sum of its parts.

But this doesn't mean that two hundred are better than two. Beyond a certain point, numbers become counterproductive. It's very difficult to get a large group of people to harmonise energy and intention for a particular purpose. This is one (I think the most significant) reason why covens limit their number to thirteen—twelve plus the High Priestess. Controlling and directing energy in a group larger than that is just too difficult for most people to manage.

I find even twelve people can be a bit unwieldy. Eight seems to be a good number, and some of the most powerful workings I've been involved in have used only three—two women and a man, or two men and a woman.

The other thing is that the larger the group, the harder it becomes to develop the bonds of love and trust ('perfect love and perfect trust') which is both necessary to group work and an outcome of it. The sense of companionship that can develop in a working group is a great joy. It's a friendship closer than family. Conversely, if things go wrong, and magical work acts as a pressure cooker to individual frailty and unresolved issues, the hurt and sense of loss goes that much deeper.

So you need to be very discerning when you're looking for a group to work with. Don't rush in just because somebody's placed an ad in *Pagan Times* saying 'Coven open to new members.' The most important—and difficult—thing about group work is finding the right group.

I very often advise people to set up their own group with one or two like-minded friends who are at about the same level. Call it a study group, make a commitment to meet regularly (say, every full moon) for a year and a day. You might choose a book to study (see the booklist—*The Spiral Dance* and *Positive Magic* are very good for this). Discuss matters spiritual and magical, and see where the Goddess wants you to go.

If you do decide to set up a working group, it's important to take time to build up mutual trust. Make sure you're in agreement on principles and ethics. Ask yourselves what your purpose is. If it's simply to have a bit of slightly naughty fun spellcasting or charm-making, by all means go ahead. But the group won't last, and the break-up is likely to fracture friendships. Serious magic is serious business.

Chapter Three

you light up my life: candle and colour magic

Candle magic is at once the most simple and the most complex of the magics.

It is simple because it is one of the oldest and apparently easiest of the magics. We light candles to bring the glow of romance or special occasion to a dinner table. We put a night-light in a child's room to ward off the night terrors. We light a candle to help us focus in meditation. We may dedicate a votive candle in a church to someone's healing, or to light the path to Heaven for a departed loved one. The first step in any ritual work is to light what's known as the Presence or Spirit candle.

Strike a match, touch it to the wick, and there you are. Instant light. But pause a moment.

'*Fiat lux*' (Let there be light) said the Lord God, and there was a light on the moving waters of the deep, and life began to emerge on to dry land. To be able to create light has until quite recently been a mysterious and intensely magical act.

Fire itself remains an object of caution, fear and, in many cultures, reverential awe. Our earliest stories tell how a hero stole fire from Heaven (like the Greek Prometheus), or how a benevolent goddess (the pre-Celtic Brigid) showed humanity the use and keeping of a sacred flame.

In magical work fire is the element associated with the will—the controlled and disciplined intent, the passion and courage needed to bring about a desired end.

But it's surprisingly difficult to maintain the necessary 'controlled and disciplined intent' without assistance for more than a very short time—just as it's difficult to control fire without a hearth or fire-pit. It's been said that a true magician can perform magic naked in a desert with no tool but the trained mind and will. For most of us, however, the mind wanders in the direction of the shopping, or tonight's television, or the new man or woman in the office or on the bus.

Lighting a candle at once helps us focus on our magical intention, and acts as a controlled source of fire—a force that lives at the heart of our solar system, that governed the making of the world, that lives in volcano and in forest fire.

Does candle magic work?

A candle is a controlled fire. And like fire, candle magic is *quick*. Any situation which requires dramatic, sudden change should respond to the lit flame.

Some friends who had moved interstate on business decided to sell their house in Melbourne. They needed a quick sale, for not less than a certain amount. They phoned to tell me that their move would be permanent, and to ask me to send a little energy towards a favourable outcome. They were planning a formal ritual at darkmoon, a day or so hence.

When they phoned a couple of weeks later, it was to tell me that the house had found a buyer, who wanted to move in immediately. Settlement was already under way. I asked what ritual they'd used—one never knows when it might come in handy! Oh, they were so tired on the night that they just lit a candle, stated what they needed and went to bed.

A fortnight (darkmoon to full moon) to put a house on the market and find a buyer is pretty good going. You see what I mean about quick.

As with any of the magical techniques, the difficult part is in deciding what it is you really want, or need.

Candle magic operates in combination with colour magic (sight) and the sense or power of smell (both related to the element of air). The candle itself is made of wax and a wick (earth element) which provide the combustible substances. The anointing oil, as a liquid, partakes of the element of water. And the lit flame (element of fire) cannot burn without the presence of air. So in a lit candle we find all four elements in balanced cooperation.

Symbolically, your will must always be grounded by your intelligence or judgement and informed by feeling.

You choose the colour of the candle and the fragrance of the anointing oil (with which you *dress* the candle) according to need—abundance, love, psychic protection, health and healing, spiritual issues.

The more simple and focused the need, the more effective the magic. But our needs are rarely simple.

Say, for instance, you decide you want to work candle magic for a new job. Do you want another job because you're bored with what you're doing, not challenged intellectually? Because you are at odds with one or more of your workmates, or your boss? Because you're not earning enough to make ends meet? These are three different issues, and your choice of candle colour will be different in each case.

If your job satisfaction depends on an intellectually stimulating environment, your job search is governed by Mercury, the planet of communication, and by the Element of Air—the element which relates to mind and wit. Your candle will be orange or yellow in colour (though it might be sky-blue—see below).

If you need a harmonious environment, Venus is the governing planet. The element is trickier—water can be a gentle stream or a raging sea. For Venus, the candle should be rose-pink or emerald green. The candle colour for the Element of Water is blue—which incidentally is also the colour associated with psychic protection.

If money is the issue, the planet is Jupiter and the colour is royal blue. The element is Earth and the colour candle is deep green—sometimes called forest green.

There is considerable variance about which colour to use. Qabalistic colour scales relate to planetary correspondences and archangelic forces. The Elemental colours are sometimes the same, sometimes different. You can, of course, short-circuit all this and use a white candle, since white contains all colours. I use a lot of white candles.

As I found when I first started work on this chapter, candle magic can get enormously complicated. You get so caught up in what colour candle, what anointing oil, what phase of the moon, what fire-god or goddess to invoke to empower your work, that it's easy to forget what you started out to do, which is to ask for help with a particular issue or problem.

Throughout this book I have suggested what colour candle might be appropriate for some particular task, or what colour cloth should be used for a certain charm. This chapter will begin to explain why and how to make that choice. But please bear in mind that these are the colour correspondences I use and have found to work for me. Other books will give different attributions. Only personal experience will teach you what works for you.

Colours and their significance

Remember that the colours given below are relevant, not only to your choice of candle in candle magic, but to your choice of coloured cloth for charm-making. The gemstone or crystal specified can be added to a charm bag to bring that energy to the charm. Because of the permanence of the stone and its intimate relationship to the Element of Earth, it helps ground or earth the charm—that is, bring about its desired outcome. It's also a particularly useful addition to a charm intended for long-term action (e.g. an abundance or protection charm).

- **White** contains all colours, so if in doubt, this is the colour to use. In the Western tradition it is also associated with purity and purity of intention. In China, however, it is the colour of mourning. In chakra work it is the colour of the transpersonal point, the connection to the divine, the High Self, the Holy Guardian Angel. The Qabalistic sephira is *Kether*, which means Crown. The gemstone is the diamond. Clear quartz crystal can however take its place.

- **Violet** is associated with spirituality and spiritual devotion. In Celtic wisecraft it is placed, together with white, in the centre of the Circle of the Elements—the place of Spirit, which harmonises, reconciles, transmutes and transforms Air and Water, Fire and Earth. In chakra work it relates to the crown chakra, the Thousand-Petalled Lotus. The gemstone is amethyst in its paler tones.

- **Purple** is the colour of majesty, sovereignty and rulership. It is a combination of red (Mars) and royal blue (Jupiter) and shares the qualities of those planets. Like violet, it is associated with the crown chakra and the gemstone amethyst (in its darker tones). In a sense, purple is the active and outgoing expression of the energy of which violet is the passive and receptive form.

- **Indigo** is sometimes called royal or sapphire blue. In chakra work it is the colour associated with the brow chakra, the centre of higher clairvoyance which is activated during meditation. It is the colour associated with Jupiter and the Qabalistic sephira *Chesed* (Mercy). It is used in abundance work when what you are seeking is a general and universal abundance, prosperity rather than a specific outcome (say, an article or a sum of money). It is also protective—this is the colour to visualise as a shield interposed between you and a known source of psychic attack. Sapphire is the gemstone. Lapis lazuli, a deep blue stone shot with gold, has been used in protective amulets since ancient Egyptian times.

- **Sky-blue** is associated with the throat chakra and the ability to express yourself freely. For this reason it is often associated with the planet Mercury and the Elemental power of Air, both of which are to do with communication. In druidic tradition it is the colour worn by the Bardic grade. The bards were the keepers and communicators of oral records, history, lore and family genealogy in Celtic society. In Christian tradition it is the colour of the Blessed Virgin. One of her titles, *Stella Maris* (Star of the Sea), points up the Elemental association with water, the element of flow and change. Light a blue candle to honour the Lady who changes everything She touches, and to facilitate communication and change in your life. The gemstone is aquamarine, but blue lace agate is also effective.

- **Turquoise** is also associated with the throat chakra. The stone itself (from which the colour takes its name) is believed to be highly protective and was used extensively in ancient Egypt with this quality in mind. It is also revered in Tibetan Buddhism and by Native American tribes (especially the Zuni, Apache and Navajo).

- **Green** is the colour of the Element of Earth and is also associated with Venus and the sephira *Netzach* (Victory).

Its associations are therefore with fertility, with material and earthly abundance, and with good luck in the short term (good fortune, long-term, is associated with Jupiter). Green is also one of the most important colours used in healing work where the object is to sustain or improve general health (as opposed to recovery after surgery, for instance). Remember how you feel when you walk barefoot through soft grass, or see a landscape dappled with a thousand different shades of green. That's the quality you are utilising when you invoke this element. The gemstone is emerald (the stone of Venus and Netzach) but both malachite and aventurine can be used in charms and amulets of Earth. They can also be worn over the heart chakra, whose colour this is, to facilitate open-heartedness or ward against too much vulnerability, as appropriate.

- **Rose-pink** is the colour associated with love as affection, with harmony and self-love. Burn a pink candle to draw love into your home and environment (but read Chapter Four for the difference between love and lust). Rose quartz is the stone of choice. Rhodocrosite can also be used, but I prefer rose quartz because of its clarity and translucence.

- **Coral** is a colour between rose-pink and yellow—a pinkish apricot—which is sometimes used in love magic as it is more grounded and grounding than rose-pink. Like turquoise, it takes its name from the mineral. Coral is sacred to Aphrodite, Greek Goddess of sexual love, and beads of coral can be added to charms or used as an amulet to attract love.

- **Yellow** is the colour of the Element of Air and is associated with the qualities of Mind, verbal wit, clarity of thought and the ability to take the long view of events.

Burn a yellow candle to bring mental clarity to bear on a situation—especially one involving a lot of emotional turbulence. Qabalistically it is associated with *Tiphareth* (which means Beauty), the balance-point and heart of Otz Chaim, the Tree of Life. In chakra work it relates to the solar plexus, which (some anatomists believe) is where *prana*, life-energy, is drawn into the body. The gemstone is topaz, but amber, rutilated quartz (with the gold inclusions known as Venus Hair) or golden tiger-eye does very well in charms and amulets.

- **Orange** is a combination of red or rose-pink and yellow. Red is associated with Mars, courage and passion; yellow with the mind and cool thought. There is an apparent conflict or contradiction here. Perhaps the function of orange is to bring wit and will, mind and passion, into balance. This certainly fits with its assignation on the Tree of Life to the sephira *Hod* (meaning Splendour or Glory) and the planet Mercury—the planet governing communication and commerce. In chakra work, orange is assigned to the belly chakra, which is associated with feeling, the emotions and clairsentience (the reception of psychic information through feeling rather than through the mind). The gemstone is citrine, but I use carnelian, an orange-coloured agate.

- **Red** is the colour of the Element of Fire and of the sephira *Geburah*, which means Severity. The planetary association is with Mars, the God of War. It is understandable therefore that this is first and foremost the colour used in protective magic. But its associations with anger as well as with courage make it tricky to handle—for me, at any rate. I had a ferocious temper as a teenager, and continue to be aware that the tiger is only tucked away taking a nap, not banished forever. Red is the colour assigned to the base or sacral chakra, which governs primal survival and the sexual drive and appetites. It's a colour often used in love magic, but I think has very little of love about it. However, if your lust life needs sparking up, a red candle is the colour for you. The gemstone is ruby or garnet, but red jasper does very nicely in charms and amulets (agates are more grounding than gemstones).

- **Black** has a very bad press in the West. It is associated with negative magic, with death and mourning. We get a better appreciation of it from Qabalah, where it is the colour associated with the sephira *Binah*, which means Understanding. Binah is at once the Great Mother and the Bitter Sea out of which all life has come and to which it will and must return. To further compound this ambivalence, the planetary association is with Saturn, the planet of constriction, whose metal is lead. But Saturn is also the planet of initiation through restriction, and of wealth through inheritance. There are times when a binding is positive—to bind yourself against a bad or destructive habit, to bind a rapist or a perpetrator of domestic violence against doing further harm, may be permissible. As always, you need to be very sure of your motives—as you bind, so you are bound. The stones are jet and obsidian.

- **Brown** is a colour associated with earth, groundedness and stability. As worn by religious orders, it symbolises humility and a death to worldly things. It is also, of course, the colour of chocolate!

- **Silver** is the colour (and metal) associated with the Moon and with the Goddess, especially as Artemis/Diana, protector of single women and small children. The associated sephira *Yesod* (Foundation) has the mixed colours of silver and violet. Silver and sky-blue are the colours of the Goddess Isis. Light a silver candle for the protection that a mother gives her children, at once fierce and tender. Light one, too, to invoke the power of imagination into your creative life. *Yesod*'s other title is 'The Treasure House of Images'. The gem is of course the moonstone but selenite (as the name suggests) can also be used.

- **Gold** is the colour (and metal) associated with the Sun and various sky-gods, especially Apollo, brother of Artemis. The associated sephira is *Tiphareth* (Beauty), and the path between it and *Yesod* is governed by the Tarot card of Temperance—which has a great deal to teach about the relationship between the sexes! Use a gold candle to invoke Apollonian clarity and light into the dark corners of your life. Many of Apollo's sanctuaries in ancient Greece were also temples of healing, and the colour gold is often used in healing wisecraft. The associated gem is the topaz.

- **Rainbow-coloured** candles and cloths do precisely what one would expect—they invoke the qualities of all the colours involved. The rainbow is a symbol of promise and of the soul in all its variety. Light a rainbow candle to help you find the gold at the end of it.

CANDLE SAFETY

- Don't leave a burning candle unattended, especially if you have children or animals in the house.

- Don't put a candle on a bookshelf or similar space unless there is *at least a metre (3–4 ft)* clearance above the flame. You risk scorching the underside of the shelf over the candle, and eventually setting it on fire.

- Make sure that the candle-holder is stable (not too tall), non-combustible and has a dish to catch any overflowing wax.

- Don't put a candle near curtains which may be blown into the flame and ignite. Fire elementals (salamanders) are notoriously mischievous!

- If you don't have a suitable (i.e. safe) place where a candle can be left burning, extinguish it and relight it when you can sit with the flame. And consider using a night-light (sometimes called a tealight) of the sort used in aromatherapy burners—pretty brass holders are readily available.

- Every house should have a fire blanket or fire extinguisher (or a bucket of sand) on hand in case of accident.

Remember the proverb we learnt as children—'fire is a good servant but a bad master'. Fire, like anger, needs control and direction to be most effective.

'Dressing' or dedicating a candle

The custom of 'dressing' a candle by rubbing it with perfumed oil is not usually explained, except as 'one of the things we do'. I suspect the practice may go back to a time when candles were most commonly made of animal fat or tallow (only churches and royalty could afford beeswax). They must have smelt like a rancid old chip-pan when lit.

We know the ancient Egyptians added perfumes to their candles and anointing oils. They are also amongst the earliest recorded users of incense. There seems to have been an understanding (perhaps taught to them by Isis, Mistress of Magics) of the power of perfumes to trigger altered states of consciousness.

From a magical point of view, anointing a candle with an appropriately perfumed oil helps charge or imbue it with your personal energy. It also helps you focus your intent—your desired magical outcome—on the candle. If the anointing is done while chanting over or be-spelling the candle, you have a kind of magical triple whammy at work.

TO PREPARE A CANDLE DRESSING OIL

✦ You can use pure concentrated oils, but it is more economical (and, I find, just as effective) to use a carrier oil such as almond or apricot to make up an anointing oil.

✦ Put a small amount (15–20 ml) of carrier oil into a suitable bottle and add 3 drops of your chosen pure essential (aromatherapy) oil or oils. Cap or cork the bottle and shake it 39 times (3 for the Triple Goddess, multiplied by 13 for the number of lunar months) while chanting:

Creature of Art, I charge thee
By the power of my will I charge thee
To the work of . . . (state your purpose—protection, healing, whatever) *I charge thee—*
So be it. So be it. So be it.

✦ Your oil is now ready for use. Be sure to label what it is for. A protection oil on an abundance candle or charm may have some interesting (and unpredictable) results.

There are different views on the method used to anoint a candle. Some say that you work from the middle of the candle out to both ends. I can't understand why—logic says you'd work from base to point, since that's where the flame is and therefore where the energy is being transmuted. Another alternative is to work in a spiral—the oldest symbol of transformation and the Goddess—again, from base to point.

You can also inscribe your intent, in words or symbols, on the side of the candle. However, if you've gone to all this trouble to choose the right colour and the right oil, I should think there's a fair chance you'll remember your original intention without the inscription. Do what feels right for you.

But be-spelling the candle—stating the specific purpose for which it is being dedicated—is a different matter. Words, especially words uttered with magical intent, have power.

This is definitely an instance when you will need to compose a personal spell for a specific outcome. The most effective spells seem to be those that have a natural rhythm and, if possible, a rhyme. Remember, this isn't intended to be great literature—but it does need to be an accurate representation of the desired outcome. Once again, the more energy you put in, the more effective your spellcrafting. Nothing is for nothing.

Below is an example of spellcrafting for a specific outcome:

CANDLE SPELL TO SELL A HOUSE

Selling anything is under the planetary influence of Mercury—so you might choose an orange candle and anoint it with one of the fragrances associated with Mercury, such as lavender. You might also put lavender bags in the cupboards and burn a lavender—perfumed aromatherapy candle when prospective buyers are coming to inspect the property. But you might think that a successful or profitable outcome is what you really want. This falls under Jupiter—dark blue candle, anointed with nutmeg, clove or cedar oil. Or you may want buyers to be impressed by the charm and beauty of the house and garden, to 'fall in love' with the place. Venus is the planet, and the oils are rose or jasmine.

✧ Having chosen candle (or candles) and oil, you *dress* the candle while chanting something like:

I draw to me a buyer
Who loves my house like me
Who's willing to go higher
To give the price I need.

✧ Then place the candle in a safe place, light it, and wait.

When you light a dressed and dedicated candle, you are reminded of your magical intention every time you see the flame. If you've chosen a long-burning candle you are also reminded every time you relight it and re-state your magical intention.

How do I know which fragrance oil to choose?

Read half-a-dozen books and you'll get six different sets of attributions to planets and elements. Perfumes are highly individual in the responses they provoke. If a particularly happy or sad time in your life is triggered in memory by a fragrance, then that outweighs anything any book, including this one, may have to tell you about planetary or elemental associations.

Note: The essential oils listed below under their elemental, planetary or astrological ruler are plant-based. They can therefore be used in their plant form in the making of charms and incenses where a particular influence or energy is needed.

AROMATICS AND THEIR ASSOCIATIONS

◎ *The Elements*

Air	Mind, wit	Galbanum, fennel, lavender, mastic, bergamot, peppermint, lime
Fire	Will, courage	Coriander, basil, cinnamon, olibanum, pepper, ginger, clove
Water	Feeling	Vetiver, verbena, dill, rose, gardenia, vanilla
Earth	Endurance	Jasmine, birch, myrrh, nard, oakmoss, clary sage
Spirit		Frankincense, lotus, Parma violet

◎ *The Planets*

Saturn	Constraint	Civet, myrrh, patchouli, cypress, vetiver
Jupiter	Abundance	Cedar, nutmeg, anise, hyssop, clove, bay laurel, sandalwood
Mars	Strength	Pine, basil, allspice, musk, coriander, oakmoss, chili, tobacco
Venus	Love	Rose, vanilla, ylang-ylang, honeysuckle, rose geranium, apricot
Mercury	Communication	Mastic, fennel, dill, lavender, citrus, bergamot, clary sage
Sun	Clarity	Cinnamon, galangal, ambergris, bay, frankincense

Moon	Intuition	Orris, camphor, jasmine, camomile, mugwort, gardenia

◎ *The Zodiac*

Aries	Coriander, pine, basil, cinnamon, tarragon, cardamom, petitgrain
Taurus	Geranium, dill, jasmine, myrtle, patchouli, vanilla
Gemini	Anise, lavender, mace, basil, mastic, bay, bergamot, peppermint
Cancer	Jasmine, aloe, lemon, orris, nard, white sandalwood, camphor
Leo	Cinnamon, nutmeg, ambergris, frankincense, allspice, bay
Virgo	Mastic, sandalwood, lavender, spearmint, fennel, bergamot
Libra	Rose, birch, cypress, spearmint, cedar, myrrh
Scorpio	Musk, pine, allspice, galangal, ginger, violet, pennyroyal
Sagittarius	Hyssop, dill, clove, aloe, cedar, pine, sage
Capricorn	Cedar, vetiver, wormwood, myrrh, bay, cypress
Aquarius	Myrrh, spearmint, pine, bergamot, cypress, eucalyptus, fennel
Pisces	Violet, patchouli, nutmeg, cedar, anise, pine

If you 'compare and contrast' these lists you will notice a number of recurrences. This is because, as any astrologer will know, the signs of the Zodiac are grouped under the four elements:

Air	Aquarius, Gemini, Libra
Fire	Aries, Leo, Sagittarius

Water	Pisces, Cancer, Scorpio
Earth	Taurus, Virgo, Capricorn

In addition, each sign has its own planetary ruler—but Venus, for example, governs both Taurus and Libra, and Mercury rules both Gemini and Virgo.

Confused? You're in good company! As you become practised, I suggest you work out your own personal set of correspondences. A good book on magical aromatherapy, such as Mary Greer's *The Essence of Magic*, will help.

If your needs are complex, or just for the fun of it, you may consider making and fragrancing your own candles. Most of us don't go to this trouble—though you will find, if you do, that your own, handmade candles carry an energy that shop-bought ones lack.

Handmade candles can be as simple or as complicated as you want. Candles rolled from beeswax 'foundation' are the easiest to make, but burn quickly and are quite expensive. Hand-dipped candles look beautiful but are time-consuming to make. However, you can, if you choose, use layers of different colours appropriate to your purpose. This is very useful if you want one candle to cover different aspects of the same outcome. Moulded candles can be made using milk cartons, yoghurt pots, and even the cardboard cylinders from toilet rolls, as the moulds. And you can add colour and an appropriate essential oil to further help focus your intent.

Why go to all this trouble when you can buy candles for minimal sums from your local supermarket? Because the more personal energy (will) you put into your magical work, the more effective it will be. Nothing is for nothing—or, more scientifically put, energy is not lost, it simply passes from one form to another (otherwise known as the Third Law of Thermodynamics).

So consider making your own candles. Craft shops will have supplies of wax, wicks and colouring materials, and there are how-to books readily available. Check your nearest adult education centre for courses and weekend workshops—a little practical advice before starting out can save hours of frustration.

But don't use a favourite saucepan to melt the wax—it will never be the same again!

GETTING STARTED

✦ Select your candle by colour and/or perfume. Your choice will be governed by the purpose, the focus of your work.

✦ Prepare—'dress'—the candle, using aromatherapy oils.

✦ Dedicate the candle—'bespelling' it to your purpose.

✦ Light the candle.

✦ Focus energy on your desired outcome.

✦ If safe to do so, allow the candle to burn out.

I'm confused. What colour candle do I need for ...?

ABUNDANCE

◎ In the sense of generalised success and prosperity—abundance of friends, having enough to be comfortable and some left over for partying—this falls under Jupiter. Deep blue candle; clove, bergamot or sandalwood oil. Abundance of opportunity, say in your job, is also covered.

- Abundance of material things, especially money and goods, relates to the Element of Earth. Burn a deep green candle anointed with oakmoss, myrtle or patchouli oil.

ACCESS TO FEELING REALM

- Element of Water. Burn a pale blue candle anointed with camphor, honeysuckle, jasmine or mugwort oils.

- Insights during dreams: a silver candle, camphor or jasmine oil.

COURAGE

- Mars, Element of Fire. Burn a blood-red candle dressed with basil, bay, clove or chili oil.

CREATIVITY

- Imaginative work, poetic insights: the Moon, sephira of *Yesod*, 'the Treasure House of Images'. Silver or violet candle, oils of camphor, mugwort, jasmine, gardenia.

- Intellectual creativity: the Sun, sephira of *Tiphareth*. Gold candle, oils of bergamot, frankincense, neroli.

FERTILITY

- Physical fertility, to encourage plants and people to grow and multiply: Element of Earth. Dark green candle; oakmoss, myrtle or patchouli oil.

- Fertility of wit, inventiveness: under Mercury. Orange candle. Lavender, lemongrass or spearmint oil.

GROUNDEDNESS

- Element of Earth. Brown candle, oils of pine, juniper, cypress, oakmoss.

HEALTH AND HEALING

- General vitality: leaf green candle, oils of lime, sandalwood, pine.

- To support after surgery or during acute infection: sky-blue candle, hyssop or sandalwood oil.

HARMONY (AT HOME OR OFFICE)

- Pink or coral candle. Rose, jasmine, ylang-ylang, apricot or vanilla oils.

LOVE AND LUST

- True love, deep affection, sincere friendship: rose-pink or coral candle, blend of rose, jasmine and oakmoss oils.

- Lust (are you sure you can handle it?): red candle, blend of damiana, oakmoss and gardenia oils—anoint each other as well as the candle.

MENTAL CLARITY

- Element of Air, the Sun: yellow or gold candle. Oils of frankincense, bergamot, rosemary, lavender, clary sage.

PSYCHIC DEVELOPMENT

- Element of Water, the Moon. Blue or silver candle. Oils of jasmine, gardenia, camomile, mugwort, Dittany of Crete.

PSYCHIC PROTECTION

- Active: Element of Fire, planet Mars, sephira *Geburah*. Blood-red candle. Oils of basil, chili, mustard, ginger, allspice, sandalwood.

- Defensive: Isis. Electric (gas-flame) blue candle. Oils of camphor, sandalwood, rosemary.

- To bind a known enemy: planet Saturn, sephira *Binah*. Black candle, myrrh oil.

SELF-LOVE AND SELF-ESTEEM

- Element of Water, planet Venus, sephira *Netzach*. Emerald-green or rose-pink candle. Oils of jasmine, rose, lotus, apple, strawberry.

SERENITY

- Element of Spirit, sephira *Kether*. Violet candle. Oils of frankincense, lotus, Parma violet.

SPIRITUAL ISSUES

Depends on the nature of the issue. For:

- Clarity: seeing your path forward—gold candle, frankincense oil

- Intuition: whether a path is right for you—silver candle, camphor or mugwort oils

- Contemplative or meditative insight: violet or purple candle. Oils of frankincense, sandalwood, Dittany of Crete.

Other uses of candle magic

I light a candle before beginning a new piece of work. It helps keep me centred, focused on what I want to achieve. It dedicates the work (and the worker) to the service of the Light and the Goddess. There is an ancient Egyptian prayer, from the *Book of the Dead* (more accurately, the *Book of Going Forth*), which I often use. Remember, whether you call it a prayer or a spell—or a blessing—is only a matter of terminology.

> *May the Light shine through us, and on us,*
> *and in us. May the wonder of life always*
> *burn bright in us. May we love, and laugh,*
> *and enter lightly into each other's hearts,*
> *May we live forever in the Light.*
>
> **Normandi Ellis, 'Awakening Osiris'**

CANDLE-MAGIC AND RELEASE WORK

The lighting of wake-fires for the souls of the dead is a very ancient custom. Bonfires were believed to light the way to the Otherworld for the departing soul, and also to protect the living from the possible ill will and resentment of the dead.

Sudden and violent death prompts in us a primeval fear (largely unconscious) that such a death may turn the beloved into a vengeful ghost. The bonfire, and now the more manageable lit candle, is symbolic of our continuing love, and of the shining and immortal spirit no longer held in the confines of mortal flesh. The candles placed at the head and foot of a coffined body are a continuance of this practice. It is significant that many of the mourners for Diana, Princess of Wales, lit candles and left them along with the more conventional flowers as a token of their grief and remembrance.

So light a candle for the departed or departing soul, whether they are close kin or the victims of some natural disaster or accident, and say:

SPELL FOR A DEPARTING SOUL

Go, beautiful soul, unto the place prepared for you
In the name of the Creator who made you
In the name of the Saviour who loves and redeems you
In the name of the Spirit that strengthens and sanctifies you
Go forth, go forth, go forth
To peace, and light, and rest, and joy,
Safe in the arms of the All-Loving.
Requiem aeternam dona eis, Domine
*Et lux perpetua luceat eis.**

And may your memory be a blessing.

* Rest eternal grant them, Lord
And light perpetual shine down upon them.

Chapter Four

all you need is love: love spells and charms

Magic is ninety-five per cent psychology, and five per cent . . . who knows?
Dion Fortune

Love magic, under the guise of popular psychology, is the backbone of a range of mainstream magazines. Articles tell you how to keep your man, how to put a spark in your love-life, how to achieve more and better orgasms. Love spells, charms, potions and philtres have become a regular feature of mainstream women's magazines. There are recipes for love charms alongside the ones for pumpkin scones.

Radio programs are in on the act too. I recently phoned my accountant, was put on hold and found myself listening to a young woman on the radio talking about a love spell involving blood and bay leaves. The person I was calling came on line before I could hear exactly what she was proposing should be done. Since bay leaves are sacred to Apollo, a god not noted for the success of his love-life, I can't imagine that the spell would be effective, except perhaps as a way of bringing rational thought into a relationship.

Many of the love spells and charms I have come across over the years range from the merely silly to the bizarre to the totally unethical. Anything involving pins and red felt or satin hearts, nail or hair clippings, and/or binding chants should immediately be put in the forty-foot-pole department. Apart from any other consideration, if you have had to compel someone to 'love' you by these means, what is that love really worth?

I should say at the outset that I have never personally cast a spell or made a charm to attract love. And I've married twice, been widowed once, divorced not at all, and have never lacked for companionship in the interim. And believe me, I'm no Elle Macpherson.

But like all women, I've had my share of duds. A man has seemed full of promise, and has turned out to be full of—well, something else entirely. And there have been times when a relationship has run its course, when there's nowhere left to go, nothing new to explore. In these situations, magic can help you extricate yourself from a wrong choice, or ease the pain of a necessary parting.

And there are times, even in a good relationship, when things don't go smoothly. The old joke about shearers and sex—'Friday too tired, Saturday too drunk, Sunday too far away'—is an all too accurate picture of busy modern life. You both get caught up in work, family and social life, and lust rates somewhere after doing the laundry, walking the dog, and watching your favourite TV show. Love is still there, all right—but lusty concupiscence has taken a seat so far back in the train that it's riding in the luggage compartment. At such times, too, magic can help restore a healthy balance to your life.

What magic should never be used for is to *compel* another's affections—or even another's lust. Many 'love' spells, as the term is generally used, are actually lust spells. They seek to bind a specific person, to compel him or her to desire you beyond all reason. It's this element of compulsion which makes them so dangerous to the user. And I don't mean just morally, ethically or karmically dangerous.

Scenario: you have met someone who is gorgeous, sexy, irresistibly cute. He (or she—same-sex attraction operates under the same rules) doesn't seem to know you exist. You decide that you can't/won't/shouldn't have to live without him, and set to with spell book and candle. You decide to make a poppet (a cloth doll)—in fact you make two, one for you and one for him. You sew a snip of your hair into yours, something belonging to him into his. You name them with your name and his. You place them heart to heart and bind them tightly together—the right colour cord, the relevant number of knots. You hide them in a secret and appropriate place, and you wait.

The next time you meet the Desired One, he notices you exist. In fact, he asks you out. Dinner, home to your place, a night of sensual passion—everything you'd hoped for. The next day, as you try to stay awake at your desk, the first of many bunches of blood-red roses arrives. He phones you that night, and the next, and the next.

Does this sound like your idea of heaven?

Take it nine months or a year down the track. He's still absolutely obsessed by you. He's also obsessively jealous. If you're not with him, then you must be with somebody else, and up to no good. He watches your house. He works out at the same gym. He drives you to work, turns up every night to collect you. He questions you about your male workmates. You can't even spend an evening with a girlfriend without provoking a fit of jealous rage. Does this still sound like heaven?

You decide you have to break the spell. You cut the cord that binds the two poppets together. But it doesn't make any difference, except that whatever obsessive love there was on his side has now turned to obsessive hate. He still wants to have sex with you, but it's marked, not by tenderness and romantic attention, but by violence and domination. And you find that the more he hates you, the harder it is for you to get out, get away. Your friends tell you to leave him, but you just can't make the break. Three years later you're still with him. Or, at worst, you've both become part of one of those murder-suicides that sometimes make the headlines.

As you bind, so you are bound. You see why I mistrust 'love spells'.

If love magic is so dangerous, this is going to be a very short chapter, right? Not necessarily. There are certain kinds of love magic that are not only acceptable, but a good thing. Remember the Doctrine of Correspondences: like calls to like.

Like calls to like

To attract love, you must be, and see yourself to be, loveworthy. Like calls to like, and love to love. All magic starts with the self. Transform the way in which you see and think about yourself, and you begin to affect the way others see you.

Where do you begin?

First of all, put a stop to negative self-talk. Too many religions teach us to despise the flesh—especially if it's female flesh. The modern litany of 'my hair looks awful . . . I'm too fat (or thin) . . . I've got a really ugly nose . . . I hate my legs and ankles' just buys into all that nonsense. The more often you say it, the more those around you will start to believe you. They won't see the whole woman, the warmth and humour and wit. It'll be a case of 'Oh, here comes That Nose again' or 'Watch out, Ugly Ankles is on her way over'.

Stop saying it, and more importantly, stop thinking it. You are a garment of the Goddess. In you She lives, moves and has her being in this world. Everything you see as an imperfection is an expression of Her infinite variety.

Learn to accept yourself as you are. It's a far more effective way to attract a partner than carrying around a mixture of patchouli leaves, hibiscus flowers, strawberry leaves, motherwort, red poppies and rose petals in a red or pink bag, as recommended recently in one magazine as a charm to attract love. (But then, some people still believe in the Tooth Fairy.)

You may engage in activities which are intended to improve your appearance or your health. Whatever you choose to do, do it for yourself. Go swimming because you enjoy it. Work out because it gives you pleasure. By contrast, dieting only makes you hungry. It's the same for the body as for the soul; needing and looking for approval—validation—from outside yourself guarantees you'll never get enough to satisfy you.

You are aiming for a state of being and feeling which makes you a joy to be near. If you spend your life expecting the world to beat you about the head and body, the world will oblige. If on the other hand you believe that life is good, most people are pretty decent and some are extraordinarily kind and loving, then that's what you will attract to you.

So how do you begin the work of transformation which will draw into your world the friends and lovers you are teaching yourself to deserve?

First you need to train yourself to feel good. That may sound strange. But a great many people spend much of their lives in a kind of emotional limbo. Ask yourself, when was the last time you felt on top of the world? Full of energy, a laugh on your lips and a spring in your step?

Now ask yourself how that day, or week, or month, went. I'll bet that you met interesting people, male and female. Maybe it was the beginning of a special friendship or a new love. You seemed to pack more enjoyment into a day than you now find in a week. Life was, in fact, pretty damned wonderful.

Remember, if you can, how that felt. Not when, or why, it ended, but how it *felt*.

That is the frame of mind and heart, the state of being, in which successful love magic is made. That is what you need to create in your life.

Invoking Aphrodite

Aphrodite is the Greek Goddess of love and pleasure, especially sexual pleasure. She enjoys and responds to the beautiful and the sensual—massage, satin sheets, silk lingerie, velvets, perfumes, comfort in all things. Her flowers are the rose, jasmine, lilac, honeysuckle, freesia—the flowers whose perfume tugs seductively at the nostrils inviting you to bury your nose in them and breathe deeply.

Friday (named after Freya, the Norse goddess of love) is the day (and night) dedicated astrologically to Venus/Aphrodite. How fortunate that her day is the end of the working week!

Make Friday evening the time to do something sensual and pleasurable. Treat yourself to a regular aromatherapy massage. It will do you more good than going to a bar or disco in search of true love, and probably cost no more.

If the budget won't stretch to a massage, go home and take a relaxing bath. Light some candles and scent the bathwater with the floral fragrances of rose or jasmine (both beloved of Aphrodite). Use a good body lotion to make sure your skin feels soft and pampered. Enjoy being with and for yourself. You are better company than most of the people you're likely to meet in a bar on a Friday night.

Don't save that silky night-dress for Mr (or Ms) Nearly-All Right. Cast the practical cotton PJs aside and tonight wear something beautiful to bed—not for someone else, but for yourself. But before you slip into bed, work the following spell.

TOUCH-AND-CHANGE SPELL

✧ Pour yourself a glass of wine. Use your best crystal, or your chalice, if you have one. The wine should be sweet and fragrant—a late-picked white, the best you can afford. If you don't drink wine, use an organic grape or apple juice instead.

✦ Sit at your dressing table mirror. Turn off any artificial lighting. Light two rose-pink candles so that they are reflected, one on either side of your face, in the mirror. Look at your face—not critically, but with love and admiration.

✦ Say:

I am a garment of the Goddess. My body is her temple, beautiful without and within. I decorate it in her honour, perfume it with her flowers. I celebrate Her rites with joy: for She has said to me and to all women, 'Behold, all acts of love and pleasure are My rituals.'

✦ Raise your glass of wine in salute to Her and to your image in the mirror. Take the first sip of wine.

✦ Look at yourself again. Say:

As I love, so I am loved. I draw to myself only those who recognise and affirm the power of love to transform all it touches.

✦ Take the second sip of wine. See the transformation already taking place as you start to accept what you have told yourself. Say:

She changes everything She touches, and everything She touches, changes.

✦ Take the third sip of wine. Say:

Change us, touch us.

✦ Sip the wine. Look again at your image, and see the Goddess looking out through your eyes. Say again:

Change us, touch us.

✦ Sip the wine. Feel Her power, which is your power, filling you. Say a third time:

Change us, touch us. And so it is.

✦ Toast your and Her image again, and finish the wine. Slip between the sheets—satin, if you have them. Dream well, sleep well, wake refreshed.

Depending on how effectively you have programmed yourself (or been programmed) to believe you're a walking disaster area, this spell will take time and repetition to be completely effective. So, having started to work on yourself and your self-belief, what else can you do?

Make your environment attractive. Don't just buy flowers for other people—buy them (or grow them) for yourself. If you spend—as many of us do—half your life in an office, make sure that your eyes fall on something beautiful during your working day. Keep a bunch of flowers on your desk. Or a single rose, to remind you of the presence of Aphrodite in your life. And make sure the flowers are fresh, and regularly replenished. Dying flowers send entirely the wrong message, and are bad *feng shui* to boot.

Now you are starting to focus on yourself, it's time to ask what you really want in a partner. Or rather, what you really need—the two can be poles apart. It's a difficult question, once you get past the 'dark hair, blue eyes, looks like Pierce Brosnan (or k.d. lang)' line of thought.

You need to think really hard about what will make you happy. What qualities are important to you? Good looks, a versatile and thoughtful lover, fidelity, a quick wit, companionship, emotional openness, shared interests and passions? Willingness to make a commitment? Loves children? Wants to get married? *Doesn't* want to get married?

Bear in mind that some of the things you think you want may not be compatible with others on your wish list. For example, if fidelity is very important to you, you may have to compromise on gorgeousness.

It may be that your sexual self-confidence is too underdeveloped to cope with a straying partner. Nothing wrong with that—just recognise and accept it. And remember that the converse isn't necessarily true. Someone who says it doesn't matter to her if her Significant Other is out tomcatting because she and her partner are mature enough to have an open relationship, may be telling the truth. Or she may have so little self-esteem that she won't make a stand for fear of losing her partner altogether.

Generally speaking, really good-looking men have many opportunities to stray and no reason not to. (They're also often poor conversationalists—they've never had to charm their way into a woman's bed.) Men with a high sex drive are easily led by their genital appendages. On the other hand, a man who wants marriage and a family may lack the element of danger you think you need to be really turned on. And so on, and so on.

Start to write down the qualities that are *really* important to you. This is an exercise in self-knowledge and can be very confronting, especially if you ask yourself why some particular quality is important, and answer yourself honestly. You may find yourself acknowledging insecurities that you might otherwise prefer to ignore. But the search for truth is the beginning of wisdom.

When you have your list, rate the qualities in order of importance. Then sit down, light a yellow candle (to aid clarity of thought), and start to write a letter.

Your letter should *not* be addressed to any specific person, no matter how convinced you are that he or she is your destined soulmate. It's a 'To Whom it May Concern', 'Dear As-Yet-Unknown', sort of letter. But it's a letter to someone you hope to meet, not a shopping list. Its tone should be personal. This is a love-letter to a stranger—though it's possible you've already met him (or her), and you haven't recognised that he or she has the qualities you've decided are important to you.

You may choose to praise him for the qualities he has—kindness, consideration, getting up first to bring you your wake-up cuppa. You may ask that he understands why you need certain things—reassurance, cuddles, lots of adventurous sex. You should describe who you are, what's important in your life—including, for example, your cat or dog. Imagine finding the perfect man and discovering that he's highly allergic to your cat, or hates dogs! If it's important that he get on well with your family, say so. Do you want (or not want) to have children? Say so!

Don't forget things like age and (if important) cultural background. If you ask simply to find your soul-mate, you may discover that he's thirty years your junior (or your senior—which doesn't give the relationship an extended shelf-life) and speaks only Mandarin or Tagalog. It may be a wonderful and fulfilling relationship. But you'll also have to deal with the inevitable stresses and strains of such a cross-cultural partnership.

Take time to get this right. What's a month or two compared to the rest of your life?

When you've got a draft you're happy with, prepare yourself and your working area for magic (see Chapter Two). The working area in this case will probably be your desk or dressing table. Have on hand a yellow, a blue and a pink candle, a red rose, some good-quality writing paper and green ink, and an envelope.

THE LOVE LETTER SPELL

✦ Set out three candles in a triangle—a yellow one on your right for clarity, a blue one on your left for change and flow, and a pink one in front of you (at the point of the triangle) for love and affection. There should be enough space between the candles for you to put the writing paper.

✦ Take time to ground and centre, focusing your mind on the work in hand. Say:

I am (your name), *a daughter of the Goddess, and I call on the Universal Love to witness and assist me in my work.*

✦ Light the candles—yellow, blue, then pink. Then write your letter out in a fair copy on good paper. Put a date on it—some months in the future, but a definite date. Sign it. Scatter some rose-petals over it, or sprinkle it with rosewater, before you fold it and put it in its envelope. Don't seal the envelope.

✦ Do this, if possible, on a new moon—the time for new beginnings.

✦ Keep the letter somewhere safe—on your altar, if you have one—where it won't be disturbed. Do not tell anyone about it.

✦ At the next new moon, take it out and read it aloud. Is there anything you want to change or add? If so, revise and update the letter, and recopy it. Burn the old one and scatter the ashes under a rose bush. If there's nothing you want to change, return the letter to its place until the next new moon, when you should read it again. And so on.

✦ As the date on the letter comes closer, be sure to keep yourself open to opportunities. Having asked the Universe for what you want, you may need to ask for the ability to recognise it and him (or her) when they cross your path!

Sometimes, before there is room in your life for a new love, you have to let go, finally and completely, of the old one. This means letting go of grief, regret and resentment, and seeing yourself as either a victim *or a victor* in the relationship. Magic can help here, too.

If you were the one to end the relationship, the one-time or would—be lover may still be hanging around. He 'just wants to be friends'. Maybe down the track a bit, with time and distance, this will be possible. But right now you both need to move on, and he's not willing to let go. You've tried kindness, you've tried open discussion, brutal honesty, even introducing him to your new love, and he's still turning up every Sunday afternoon looking like a lost spaniel. It's time for:

THE ICE-CUBE SPELL

✦ Take a slip of violet-coloured paper. Write your no-longer-lover's name and birthdate on it in black ink. Write *I release you and ask you to get on with your life.* Fold the paper small. Put it in an ice-cube container or small plastic box. Add water and a drop of myrrh oil or tincture. Put the whole thing in your freezer and leave it there. He will get the message. (He may also decide to take a trip to the Antarctic—or to Far North Queensland!) Now don't think about him!

✦ When you're certain he's well and truly gone, remove the ice-cube and bury it, paper and all, under a rose-bush.

If the separation was mutual, but painful—for example, a live-in relationship or a marriage has broken up—you may need to take more time and effort to resolve matters.

One suggestion I've heard is that you write down all the things that were wrong or that went wrong with the relationship, and why you're better off out of it. This is a kind of reverse process to the love letter spell, above; but it shouldn't be a hate letter. This is just a list, not a tirade or a plea to put things right. When you've finished your list—and cried over it, if you want and need to—roll it up, bind it with black cotton, take it outside and set fire to it. Let it burn until it is completely consumed, and let the wind take its ashes. Waning moon (dark moon) would be a good time to do this.

If you are still angry with him (or her), that anger binds you to the relationship as much as love once did. Anger can be constructive, a great source of motive energy to get you out of a destructive relationship. But the time comes when for your heart to heal you have to let the anger go. Try the following:

SPELL TO BANISH ANGER

✦ Find a nice, smooth river rock. It should be a fair size, but not so big that you can't hold it comfortably in both hands. Prepare yourself and your working area, and make sure you're not disturbed. This could get noisy.

✦ You will also need:

- a square of black silk
- a length of black thread
- a glass (or your chalice) of water
- two candles. One should be red, for your anger and for the courage that has brought you this far. The other is blue, for the emotional healing you seek and for your capacity to change and flow. Put these on your dressing table, or somewhere it will be safe for them to burn out.

✦ Sit on your bed. The two of you probably spent a lot of time there, one way and another, so it will be an easy place to prompt memory and feeling. Take the rock in your hands. Breathe on it, and say:

Powers of Air, Powers of mind, help me to see clearly what I need to know. Lift my troubles from me as a leaf flies away on the wind.

✦ Pass the rock over the red candle flame five times and say:

Powers of Fire, Powers of courage and of will, burn away my anger as a smith's fire burns away the dross in making a blade.

✦ Sprinkle a little water on the rock and say:

Powers of Water, Powers of the feeling realm, though you are soft and flowing you have shaped this rock to fit it for my purpose. Wash my sorrow from me and quench the thirst of my soul.

✧ Dip your fingers in the water and wash your eyes with it. Take a sip and drink it down.

✧ Hold the rock close to your heart. Say:

Powers of Earth, Powers of endurance, help me endure what I must and emerge triumphant, healed and whole again.

✧ Now hold the rock in your lap and focus on pouring into it all your grief, anger and sense of loss and betrayal. Feel it becoming heavy with the weight of your emotions. Shout and rage if you can or must. Weep for what's gone and cannot be reclaimed. You will or should feel quite exhausted by the end of this process.

✧ Wrap the rock securely in the black silk and bind it with the black thread. Place it between the two candles, which should be left to burn out. Sleep well, purged and free of your anger. As soon as possible next day, go to a bridge over a deep flowing river, and throw the wrapped rock into the water (check for passing oarsmen first!). Say:

Water shaped thee, water take thee,
Grief and anger I cast from me.
Fiat, fiat, fiat lux. (Let there be light)

✧ Walk away, and do not look back. Again, waning or dark moon would be an auspicious time for this work.

In some ways, closure after a live-in or de facto relationship is more difficult than if the two of you had been married. The legalities of divorce proceedings give both of you time to get used to not being a couple. And the divorce papers themselves mark the end of the legal relationship. You also have a wedding ring which you can dispose of as a final breaking of the link with your ex.

In a de facto relationship, there may be property matters to be settled or children to be protected. But there is no quitclaim, as with the decree absolute, to say *Enough! Done! Finished!* Here is a Cutting Connections Spell. You can of course use it if you are married and still waiting for your divorce—or even after the divorce has come through, if you feel it would be helpful.

CUTTING CONNECTIONS SPELL

✥ You will need:

- a photograph of you and your former partner—full-length if possible
- sharp scissors
- two envelopes
- a violet or purple candle
- a red felt-tip pen
- a single rose
- a mantelpiece or window-ledge you can use undisturbed.

✥ Prepare yourself and your working area in the usual way. Light the candle and say:

This is the time of parting. This is the time I have chosen to separate myself finally from (your former partner's name). *I do this for the good of all, and to allow us both to go forward on our separate paths.*

✦ With the red felt-tip pen, mark a line between your two bodies on the photograph. Say:

This is the line that has linked our lives.

✦ Take the scissors and cut carefully along the line you have marked until the photograph is in two pieces. Place the two halves side by side, but with a gap between them, on the window-ledge or mantelpiece. Say:

(Name), *I let you go, I release you to your own destiny and I go to mine. What was between us is finished. This is my wish, this is my will. So be it.*

✦ Place the candle in the space between the two halves of the photograph, then blow it out.

✦ The following night, light the candle, repeat *I let you go, I release you*, and move the pieces of the photograph further apart. Repeat for a further five nights (seven nights in all). By this time the halves of the photograph should be at the opposite ends of the window-ledge or mantelpiece, and the rose will have faded. Keep the petals.

✦ Time the seven days, if you can, to take place in the moon's last quarter, so that the final separation occurs at dark of the moon.

✦ Take one of the envelopes and address it to him—typewritten, not handwritten. (It matters that there should be as little personal connection as possible. It would actually be possible, if the address were handwritten, to use it to send negative magic back to the sender. The typewriter acts as a kind of *cordon sanitaire*.) There must be no indication of who has sent it. Pick up the half of the photo that has the image of your former love, and put it in the addressed envelope. Add some of the faded rose petals. Apart from the obvious symbolism, this sends the message that the divided photo is not an act of negative magic. This protects you from possible comeback and ill will.

✧ Seal the envelope, stamp and post it. If you don't know his address, send it Poste Restante to your central post office. It will either reach him eventually or end up in the Dead Letter Office, which is appropriate. **NB:** do not burn or otherwise destroy his half of the photo. Bad karma!

✧ Place the other half of the photo—your half—in the other envelope, add the rest of the rose petals, put it away and forget about it. When you find it again, some months or years later, you'll wonder what all the fuss was about.

If your marriage has ended in divorce, you may be wondering what to do with your wedding ring. One friend gave hers to a tree on the property she and her former husband had owned. It's probably still hanging there, unless some sharp-eyed bower bird has purloined it. Another threw hers into the nearest rubbish bin on her way out of the divorce court—that had been a very unhappy marriage.

You can use the Four Elements to put a ritual end to past unhappiness.

- Giving the ring to a river or the sea returns it symbolically to the feeling realm to be cleansed. As the water washes over it, so your hurts are washed away.

- Burying the ring at the base of a tree gives it back to the element of which it was made. It's also some small payment back to the planet for the depredations of the mining industry.

- Melting the ring in a hot fire destroys its shape and so its symbolic meaning. You can take it to a manufacturing jeweller—cut it in two with a pair of pliers first, if you wish. Or you can put it, in an earthenware dish, into a bonfire or hearth fire. The dish ensures that it won't fall into the ashes and keep its shape. The fire, of course, needs air in order to burn, so that uses two of the elements in purification.

If you don't want to see good gold go to waste, flatten the ring with a hammer (good for getting rid of surplus anger) and then drop it into a church poor box. Or, as a cynical and thrifty friend of mine suggested, cut the ring in two (leaving the hallmark intact) and sell it to a jeweller for its scrap value. Put the money (it won't be much) towards a massage, perfume or some expensive chocolates. You are now a free woman, and the world is your oyster.

Which leads me to:

Oysters, asparagus and all that jazz: about aphrodisiacs

There, that got your attention! No, sorry, there is no safe quick-fix solution, no 'instant lust—just add champagne and stir' powder. But some foods, herbs and spices have a long-standing (if you'll pardon the phrase) reputation as aphrodisiacs.

Often this is due to our old friend, the Doctrine of Correspondences. The perky and upright shape of a cucumber, a spear of asparagus or a stick of celery makes it easy to understand their reputation as provokers of male ardour. Casanova recommended celery.

CASANOVA'S CELERY TONIC

✧ Put four sticks of fresh celery in a pot of boiling water and let steep for twenty minutes. Add a chopped clove of garlic, a sprinkle of black pepper, a sprinkle of cinnamon and a dash of nutmeg. Stir in a good dollop of honey. Cover, and allow to stand until cool. Strain. Take a small glassful every three hours.

I don't know if it will improve a man's performance, but it should help his kidneys (celery is a natural diuretic) and be good for his arthritis.

Many foods with a reputation as aphrodisiacs gained their renown because they improved nutrition, and therefore performance. Oysters, for example, are rich in zinc. In areas in which the soil is poor in zinc, healthy development of the sexual organs in young males is impaired. Zinc is also a component of semen. So if you want to galvanise your man into action, feed him oysters—*au naturel*, of course. If you are *au naturel* yourself at the time, so much the better.

Seafood is generally rich in iodine as well as zinc. Iodine is essential to the healthy functioning of the thyroid gland, which controls body metabolism. Fatigue, lethargy, loss of interest in sex, feeling cold and a slowed pulse are signs of an underactive thyroid. 'I'm sorry, I'm just too tired' may respond favourably to *moules marinière* or a nice piece of orange roughy in shrimp sauce.

Seafood comes from the sea. The word *Aphrodite* means 'the sea-born one' or 'born of the sea foam'—so maybe the ancient Greeks knew more about nutrition than we give them credit for!

At various times, people have also given aphrodisiac credit to:

- tomatoes—once called 'love apples';
- chocolate—the Incas swore by it, and chocolate drinking was considered a sign of moral degeneracy well into Victorian times;
- honey—hence the honeymoon;
- ginger, cumin, cinnamon, peppermint, cloves, coriander, pepper, chili—all under the planetary influence of Mars, who in his Greek form as Ares was the lover (though not the husband) of Aphrodite;
- powdered rhino horn (I think you should have to catch your own rhino and ask him *very* nicely.);
- tiger testicles (see rhino horn. If you want them, you should have to collect them!); and

a host of other foods, both improbable and bizarre.

There are herbs that are used as nervines and male tonics—damiana, ginseng, saw palmetto, kola nut. I recommend that you consult a sympathetic herbalist on these. Don't try to slip them unnoticed into your husband's or boyfriend's cuppa—they taste, like many herbal concoctions, pretty vile. It's also unethical on your part, and could be dangerous to your partner.

There are other, more notorious 'aphrodisiacs'. But I feel it would be unethical for me to name them, even if only to say 'don't try them if you value your health'.

Sarsaparilla, on the other hand, is safe, a natural source of the male hormone testosterone, a blood tonic and a refreshing drink in hot weather. But you need to look for genuine Jamaican sarsaparilla root or cordial—commercial soft drinks are mainly flavoured with liquorice and aniseed. Again, the tincture may be obtainable through your herbalist.

'The sweet smell of ...'

Most women, and a lot of men, are turned on by fragrances. These are indeed genuine aphrodisiacs. Perfumes and aromas act on the limbic brain, the most primitive part of that very sophisticated system.

But response to smells is a very personal thing—association plays such a large part. Just about everybody loves the smell of jasmine, but if for you the scent of jasmine is connected to an experience of fear or sexual abuse, your response will be irrevocably coloured by that experience.

Books on aromatherapy are your best bet here. For me, the fragrance of oakmoss has an unmistakably male allure. It's the basis of a popular (and inexpensive) aftershave. Jasmine is a relaxant, useful for women suffering from performance anxiety (yes, guys, we get it too!). Any of the edible smells—strawberry, apricot, peach, orange, lime—tend to appeal to men. If someone could perfect essential oil of home-baked bread or apple pie, they'd make a fortune!

But the best aphrodisiac is a firm belief in your own sexual desirability.

Lotions, potions, charms and philtres

There was once a famous French courtesan called Ninon de l'Enclos. She lived to be eighty—no mean feat in the eighteenth century—and had devoted lovers right to the end of her life. She attributed her success and her power to captivate men (and women) to a special pleasure bath.

NINON DE L'ENCLOS' PLEASURE BATH

✦ Take a handful of:

- lavender flowers
- rosemary
- mint
- crushed comfrey root
- thyme
- celandine

✦ Put into an earthenware crock, pour one litre (one quart) of boiling water over, cover and leave to stand for twenty minutes. Strain, pour the clear portion into a warm bath, soak yourself for fifteen to twenty minutes.

The only thing that surprises me is the omission of rose petals. Comfrey is a soothing plant (demulcent) which heals scratches and abrasions, and celandine is an astringent. You'd come out of such a bath feeling taut, toned and terrific. And smelling pretty delicious, too. In an age where most people (including the aristocracy) took a bath once a year whether they needed it or not, smelling clean and fresh would be a) unusual, and b) appetising.

Many of the old herbal love charms and potions may have owed their effectiveness, not to their astrological correspondences, but to the simple fact that they sweetened the breath and helped dispel body odours.

Louise Huebner's (the author of *Power Through Witchcraft*) true love tea is in this category. She recommends that you take any blend of tea and spike it with nutmeg, rosemary, thyme, rosebuds, honey and lemon leaves. 'This chemical combination has all the witching ingredients it takes for attracting a true love.'

Yeah, right. What you have is an effective breath and stomach freshener. It will do you no harm—though you should be cautious about the quantity of nutmeg you use—but it is not of and in itself magical. If, however, you believe that drinking it (beginning, she instructs, on an odd-numbered day and continuing every night for six weeks) will make you irresistible, it might just work. But the magic lies in your belief, not in the love philtre.

Valerie Worth, in *The Crone's Book of Words*, gives a recipe for a love potion 'for one whose love you would excite and warm' which is essentially a recipe for mulled wine. She instructs you to take a gill (about 250ml) of good red wine, and add to it a teaspoon each of rosemary, anise, cloves, clear honey and orange rind, with a pinch of cumin and three green leaves from a rose-geranium. Put in a pot, bring to the boil and simmer while you count to a hundred. Allow to cool (this further infuses the spices) then strain. Warm it again before serving. She adds 'It shall not fail, unless performed by one whose heart and household keep slatternly habits'—a very neat get-out clause.

This philtre would make a very pleasant drink for a cold winter's night. I'd probably add more red wine or a shot of brandy to the mix before serving it, because the infusing process would remove most or all of the alcohol from the wine. I'd also double the quantity, so there's enough for both of you to take a loving cup. Add an open fire, a comfy sofa and a pile of soft cushions and you have the kind of love potion of which I entirely approve.

Charms, amulets, talismans ...

Love charms generally contain aromatics which will be activated by the warmth of your body—most recipes suggest you carry them on your person (read, tucked between your breasts). Like Ninon de l'Enclos' pleasure bath, they probably owed much of their effectiveness to their function as a deodorant and fragrancer.

The recipe I cited earlier, containing patchouli leaves, hibiscus leaves, strawberry leaves, motherwort, poppy petals, rosebuds and rose oil, mixed together with orris root (a fixative), would make an excellent potpourri. Sewn into a charm bag it would smell pleasant and probably give you a restful night's sleep as well. But its effectiveness in finding you your one true love is pretty limited.

An amulet or talisman of Venus/Aphrodite should be made of copper, which is her metal. I have seen for sale copper ankhs (to be worn as a pendant) which combine the energies of Venus and Isis. I have also seen copper talismans which claim to be talismans to attract love. As I am unfamiliar with the symbology used, I can't judge how effective they would be. Again, I would suggest that their effect is on the perception of the wearer rather than as a result of any innate power.

If you can find them, beads of copper, rose quartz, aventurine and coral—seven of each, and strung in that order—would make a very effective and pretty amulet. It would also be unusual enough to draw the attention of a sympathetic male—and you then have the advantage of being able to explain the symbolism as a springboard to further conversation.

Once you've done the work involved in, for example, the Letter Spell, you should be well on the way to finding the right partner with whom to share your life. But you may need an ongoing reminder of your own loveworthiness and desirability Put together an:

APHRODITE CHARM

❖ You will need:

- a piece of emerald-green velvet (Aphrodite's colour, and fabric) large enough to hold:
- rosebuds (of course!)
- jasmine flowers (naturally!)
- seaweed (She is the Foam-Born One)
- a piece of copper (Aphrodite's metal), heart-shaped if possible
- a small piece of tumbled rose quartz (for self-love)
- ditto of aventurine (the Gambler's Stone—helps you take lucky risks)
- a small piece of coral or a coral bead
- copper-coloured thread to tie or sew the charm

❖ I always add, to every charm:

- sugar for sweetness—in this case, honey would be better, but sticky!
- salt for savour (sea salt in this case)
- sesame for opening doors

❖ Place the ingredients in the velvet and secure with the thread—you can sew it into a little pillow or tie it like a Christmas pudding. If you tie it, it should be tied with seven knots—the number associated with the sephira *Netzach* (meaning Victory), whose planetary ruler is Venus.

❖ Now you need to empower—en-chant—the charm. After your usual preparations, light a green or rose-pink candle. You can make up your own chant, use

'She changes everything She touches, and everything She touches, changes'—or try the following:

Rosebud petals and sea weed
Jasmine, copper, coral bead
Rose quartz for the wounded heart
Gambler's stone for my new start
Seven tokens of Her favour
With sugar, salt for added savour
And sesame to open doors
All things chosen by Her laws
Sweet Aphrodite, Golden One!
In emerald cloth the charm is held
And seven times the charm is spelled
It is done! It is done! It is done!

✦ Repeat this seven times, while holding the charm in your hands to empower it. You have the blessing of Aphrodite. Use it well and honour Her in your life henceforth.

Whatever you do, remember the rules of love magic:

- Do not manipulate, do not coerce.
- As you bind, so you are bound.
- Do not confuse love and lust.
- Learn to love yourself first. All else follows.
- Like calls to like, and love to love.

- The magic is in you, not in spells, charms or potions.
- The greatest aphrodisiac is your belief in your own desirability.

Chapter Five

how to have it all: abundance magic

A couple of years ago a friend and I noticed that a new shop had opened nearby, selling crystals, books and similar New Age impedimenta. Curiosity drew us inside. Amongst the overpriced amethysts and 'How to Channel Dolphins' tapes there was a terracotta pipe holding several lengths of pre-loved bamboo. Attached to one end of each weatherworn length were a couple of feathers, a small crystal, and (I seem to recall) a seashell. They were labelled 'Abundance Wands'.

My friend, a card-carrying cynic, said that he was sure they were very effective in drawing abundance—to the maker. What some tatty bamboo and a few accessories would do for the buyer was make them twenty dollars poorer, and certainly no wiser.

It has been said, by wiser women than I, that it takes as much hard work to get something by magical means as it takes to get it by ordinary means (i.e. with cheque or credit card).

The only real difference is that magic may be quicker, and is probably more fun.

Of course, if you buy an abundance wand and deeply and sincerely believe that it will draw abundance to you, then it probably will—by altering your perception, improving your ability to see the abundance already present in your life.

Magic is the art of changing consciousness in accordance with will.

Abundance is one of the areas of wisecraft—and life—that is most influenced, positively or negatively, by our perception of where we are in relation to what we want or need.

We all know people who are always crying poormouth. 'I had a tiny win on the lottery—it was only a few hundred bucks, not enough to pay off Bankcard.' 'His mum gave us her sofa. All right, it's leather, but she's had it at least a year.' 'We can't afford a real holiday this year—just a week at the coast.'

We also know people who view life itself as a great gift, and anything else as a bonus. They're the ones who are likely to be saying 'I ran into this really nice woman who's doing a massage course and needs people to practise on. Free massages—just what I need!' 'Hey, the take-away has given us free samosas with our order.' 'That silly ornamental fountain I've been looking at—the shop has just knocked fifteen dollars off the price.'

Is your cup half-full or half-empty?

It is an interesting fact that once you start to expect abundance in your life, the Universe will oblige. Trust me, it's true. But this mindset is quite difficult to achieve. There is a dualism, an either/or, at the heart of Western culture. We are conditioned to think 'If you win, I lose'. We've been taught to believe that there isn't enough—love, food, money, pleasure—to go around, and we have to struggle and fight for our little bit of it. We've been told that it is greedy, sinful or just wrong to believe that we deserve anything, let alone the best.

Poverty-consciousness surrounds most of us from a very early age, and it's not surprising that so much of it rubs off on us.

And yet most babies in our society have enough to eat and drink. Most mothers love their children and want the best for them. They may not handle the stresses of mothering very well all the time, and some may handle them very badly most of the time. There are, we know, horrific cases of mistreatment of children. Physical and sexual abuse are much more common than we have previously admitted. But cruelty to a baby or toddler still causes a public outcry, a rush of revulsion that indicates to me that our society is at heart good and caring. We donate massively to charitable appeals, at home and abroad. If we were really as callous and self-centred a society as we are sometimes portrayed, we would simply shrug and say 'One less mouth to feed. All the more for me.'

However, even babies who have been loved and nurtured from conception onwards come, at some point, to get the message that the Universe doesn't in fact revolve around them and their needs. The point at which this happens, and how the crisis is handled by a baby's parents, may determine how easy it is for the adult to replace poverty-consciousness with abundance-consciousness. The younger the infant and the harsher the lesson, the more difficult it is to overcome the conditioning. Difficult—but not impossible. Recognising the nature of the problem goes part-way to resolving it.

You need to go back to that early time and reassure the child-self that it survived, flourished and knew happiness.

Denise Linn, internationally acclaimed author, lecturer and healer, tells a lovely story about herself in this regard. When she was twelve years of age her parents moved states. As an adult she realised during meditation that the trauma of moving was inhibiting her life in present time. She cast her memory back and had a recollection of herself, just before the move, sitting on a swing in their old yard, feeling utterly miserable and alone. In imagination her adult self went up to that child-self, hugged her, and told her everything would be fine—she'd make new friends and have a good life. She later went back to revisit the memory and 'remembered' that her twelve-year-old self had felt that warm reassurance and comfort at the time.

You may well ask how we can affect something that has already happened, that is 'in the past', except by going into psychotherapy for an extended period and resolving the issues involved. That is certainly one way to go, and for deeper traumas, perhaps the most effective.

But bear in mind that time is simply a human construct, something that we impose on events to give them an order we can comprehend. We speak about time as though it were linear, as if past-present-future were a straight line. It's more like a spiral, or a wheel. Everything happens in relation, not to the straight line, but to the heart of the spiral, the hub of the wheel. This is the place of Spirit, not constricted by time and space, where all is possible. Magic lies in the belief in an infinitude of possibilities.

So where do we begin? We use our imagination, the most powerful tool of magic, to go back in time. We adjust our perception of that earliest awareness of lack and limitation. Starhawk, in *The Spiral Dance*, has a process that she calls 'A Spell to Know the Child Within'. It's a good place to start. I have adapted and extended it.

BEGINNING ABUNDANCE-CONSCIOUSNESS: SPELL TO HEAL OLD HURTS

✧ You will need:

- a green and/or a blue candle (for healing of body or soul)
- a doll or soft toy—if you still have one you owned as a child, so much the better

- salt water and sweet (unsalted) water
- a sprig of rosemary (to help you remember)
- honey or a sweet biscuit
- a white cloth—silk if you can find it
- lengths of blue and green embroidery silk

✧ Sit facing south (the quarter of courage and will) and light the candle, saying:

Powers of Fire, give me courage to move beyond this old pain. Help me consume it in the fires of transformation.

✧ Focus on an incident in your early life which caused you great pain—a moment of rejection, a hurtful word or action that comes to mind when you're tired or depressed. Try to get in touch with that feeling. Uncomfortable as it is, you need to experience it again, however briefly, for the spell to be effective.

✧ Take up the doll or toy, and say:

You are a symbol of the child I was. I name you . . . (Use your childhood pet name or nickname).

✧ Using the sprig of rosemary, sprinkle it with the salt water and say:

This salt water is a token of the tears I shed.

✧ If you were unable to cry then and wish to do so now, for the hurt child you once were, do so. When you are ready, take up the sweet (unsalted) water and say:

This sweet water washes away grief and sorrow.

✦ Sprinkle the doll or toy with the sweet water, and bathe your eyes with it.

✦ Then pick up the doll or toy and cuddle it to you. Croon to it, rock it, sing it a lullaby. Talk to it. Tell it everything you would have liked to hear as a child—that it/you are smart, pretty, popular, whatever. Let it talk to you and tell you how it feels and what it wants. Listen, and remember. This part may be really difficult to do—but give it your best shot. You may now be able to satisfy some of those needs.

✦ Now visualise clear green healing energy coming up from the Earth-Mother to surround and enfold you. Hold the feeling of loving nurturance a moment. Then project that energy into the doll or toy, who is your own child-self. Create an image of your child-self as you would have liked it to be, and again project the energy into the doll, into your child-self. The light may change colour—to clear blue, white or perhaps rose-pink. Continue until you can see, in your mind's eye, the doll glowing with light and love.

✦ Take up the sweet biscuit or the honey. Say:

This is the sweetness of our life from this time onwards, rich in love, laughter and all good things.

✦ Touch it to the doll's lips and then your own. Eat the biscuit or taste the honey—licking it from your fingers as a small child would. Enjoy the moment. Say:

Abundance of love, of joy and healing
More than enough for you and me
More than enough for everyone
Filling the Universe. So let it be.

- When you are ready, kiss the doll. Then take it and wrap it in the white cloth. Say:

I wrap you close to keep you safe.

- Wind the blue and green embroidery threads around the wrapped doll, saying

I wind you round with love and healing.
As you are, so am I—
Surrounded by love and healing light.
So be it. So be it. So be it.

- Put the doll on your altar or other safe place. Take a soothing bath (jasmine would be a good fragrance to use) and go early to bed. This is hard work. Be gentle with yourself.

This spell may be repeated, as often as you need or want to. The further back into memory you are able to go on each occasion, the greater will be the healing change.

Please note that if you are a survivor of childhood sexual abuse, parts of this spell may be very difficult for you. Don't give yourself a hard time because you can't manage the visualisation, or if you feel so overwhelmed with grief that you can't go on. Do as much as you can. Try to complete the spell, even if you feel you're just walking through it. The magic will begin to work on the subtle levels. You can help it, and yourself, by talking to a counsellor specialising in this area.

There are no setbacks—only unrealised opportunities

Once you start to adjust your perception of abundance, and start to look for the half-full rather than the half-empty cup, you will find instances, both small and great, of universal benevolence.

A friend goes out of her way to find a special book you've heard about but haven't been able to track down. Another sends over a portable CD player and some CDs because you're going into hospital and will need the healing power of music. Another leaves the much-loved country of his birth to be with you because failing eyesight means that you need his loving support close at hand. These are true riches.

This book came about because of a setback that I turned into an opportunity. As the result of a misunderstanding or breakdown in communication, I lost a writing job on which I'd been counting. Apart from anything else, it represented a substantial loss of income. After spending a day or two fuming, I thought 'OK, you've got ten weeks off. Bonus. The Goddess must have thought you needed the break more than the money. What would you really like to do?' Something that's going to last more than five minutes into the next TV program, was my answer. I spoke to my agent, who said 'Why don't you write a book about spells and such? You'll have fun and I'm sure I can get a commission for you.' Rachel, my dear, a thousand thanks.

Ingredient X—the expectation of abundance

We've all at some time eaten delicious food, asked for the recipe, then tried to recreate it at home. Somehow, it never tastes quite the same. It's as if some small but vital ingredient is missing—a pinch of salt or sugar, a dash of this or that. It may be a matter of technique, or something as ephemeral and unrepeatable as the atmosphere created by the friends gathered at that particular time and place. But Ingredient X just isn't there.

The secret ingredient in all abundance spells and charms is the expectation of abundance. You need above all to focus, not even on the half-full cup, but on the Cauldron of Plenty, full to overflowing with all good things. With that as a given, let's look at some nuts-and-bolts magic-making.

Valerie Worth, in *The Crone's Book of Words*, has a splendid spell for success on important occasions.

FOR SUCCESS ON IMPORTANT OCCASIONS

✦ Take three or four or five of the following: marigold, celery, mint, grass, nasturtium, fennel, cress. They must be fresh and green. Tie in a bundle and steep in a bath until the water is tinged green. Lie in the water and repeat three times:

I shall bathe
And I shall be
As green and strong,
Good herbs, as thee.
Draw me favour
Draw me fame
Draw bright honour
To my name.

If you are going for a job or promotion and you know that you are in competition with one other person, it is *not* legitimate to hope something nasty happens to them on the way to the interview. It is, however, quite in order for you to work to enhance your own chances. You may also work for them to be offered a better job elsewhere, thus leaving the field clear for you.

This is also a good and ethical way to deal with a workmate who is making life difficult for you and others. Just light a violet candle and ask the Universe to find them a job suited to their talents and abilities, in another company—'for the good of all and according to the free will of all'. If you're feeling naughty or really put-upon, you can ask that it be in another town or state—but remember the Law of Threefold Return and be prepared for your firm to tell you that the promotion you want involves a move interstate or overseas.

CHARM TO GET A JOB

This one is from Starhawk's *The Spiral Dance.*

✦ Take a square of green cloth, and put in it bay laurel, lavender, and High John the Conqueror root. Add four other herbs governed by:

- Mercury—for a job involving communications or commerce
- the Moon—for a job involving healing, women's work or health, psychology
- Jupiter—for a job involving leadership and responsibility, or the law
- Mars—for a job requiring aggressive, assertive action
- the Sun—for a job outdoors, in agriculture or nature, or an easygoing, enjoyable job
- Venus—for a job requiring charm and persuasion—hotel manager, telephone sales

- Saturn—for architecture, history, or any job where you will be limiting others' actions or freedom (police work, for example).

Add a silver coin, for wealth, and pictures of any important tools you use in your work. Tie it with purple thread.

Bay laurel is under the influence of the Sun, lavender under Mercury (to facilitate communication) and High John under Jupiter (the planet governing business success). You'll find the other herbal correspondences you need in the tables of aromatics and their rulers in Chapter Three.

I would recommend be-spelling the charm by kneading it in your hands while chanting something like:

Sun, Jupiter, and Mercury
Trine of planets, be with me
As I seek and ask and read
Help me find the job I need.
Other herbs here gathered, aid
The search for work that is well-paid
And satisfies my need to be
Fulfilled in what I do for fee.

This would be a good charm to make when you want to improve your present job, as well as when you need to find new employment. Carry it in your bag when you're going to an interview. Sleep with it under your pillow for dream-insights into overlooked opportunities. Every morning, press it in your palms and breathe in the smell of its contents. Or put it on your altar to work for you at all times.

Now get out there and start looking! Magic isn't a substitute for work. It's not about sitting back and waiting for the world to beat a path to your door. Beat the path yourself by reading the employment ads and updating your résumé. It's not called magical *work* for nothing!

Sometimes you have to get past first base with a written application in order to get the interview. You will of course have done the work of putting together (or having a professional service put together) a good résumé. But it still has to get into the right hands. Try the following. It's another of Valerie Worth's.

FOR THE EFFICACY OF AN IMPORTANT LETTER

❖ Write the letter, and seal and stamp it. Then put it on a table, on a black velvet cloth. Pour salt around it in a circle of silver, then say:

Words that run
Before my pace
And carry me
Beyond this place,
Please the eyes that greet thee next
And work my will
Within thy text.

❖ Fold the cloth to cover the letter, and kiss it three times. Then carry the letter immediately to the postbox and post it.

So you've got the job of your dreams, and now you have to come up with the goods. You're worried about whether you over-sold yourself. Accept that you didn't. The job may stretch you, but if it were beyond your abilities you wouldn't have got it. How do you bolster or enhance your ability and belief in yourself? Try the following.

Charm or perfume oil for creative work

It's important, if you possibly can, to wait for the appropriate phase of the moon for this work. Choose:

- New or waxing moon, for beginning a project

- Near full moon, for inspiration

- Waning moon for productive self-criticism, reworking.

Now choose which element is appropriate for the work in hand.

- Air for mental work, especially work involving words or clear communication.

- Earth for crafts and work with the hands

- Fire for creative energy, the will and enthusiasm to get things done

- Water for emotional expression.

Now check out the table *Aromatics and their Associations* in Chapter Three and choose the herbs or oils you wish to use (or have on hand). Remember that, while a charm is mainly composed of herbs or spices, it's all right to use some essential oils (e.g. bergamot oil) if you don't have the herbs. You also don't need to use all the herbs listed.

A **charm of Air** may contain fennel, lavender, mastic, cassia, bergamot oil, peppermint and lime. (Buy a lime, peel it and dry the skin—a short time in a microwave will do this quickly). Add a bird's feather to give the charm (and your thoughts) wings. Tie in a *yellow* cloth with silver thread. You may want to add a crystal or a piece of tumbled quartz to 'fix' or ground the charm. Fluorite is the stone closely associated with mental clarity.

To make the **perfume oil** choose compatible fragrances (cassia, bergamot and lime oils, for instance) or a single fragrance such as lavender, and add a few drops to a small amount of carrier oil such as apricot or almond oil.

A **charm of Earth** may contain some or all of: jasmine, myrrh, oakmoss, clary sage and pine. Add a pinch of salt and a few grains of rice or wheat. Tie in a *green* cloth with a brown thread. The crystal is aventurine (for luck) or malachite (for grounding). Jasmine and oakmoss, or clary sage and pine, are the blends for your perfume oils.

A **charm of Fire** may contain: coriander, basil, cinnamon, clove, chili pepper, ginger and frankincense. Tie in a *red* cloth with an orange thread. The crystal is garnet or red jasper—unless you happen to have a spare ruby knocking about. Wear the essential oils as single fragrances—though cinnamon, clove and coriander, with the addition of neroli or sweet orange oil, would be a pleasant combination.

A **charm of Water** may contain: vetiver, mugwort, verbena, rosebuds, dill and vanilla (get the whole bean from a good deli or cooking supply shop—don't use vanilla essence). Dittany of Crete (a scrying herb) will add insight to the charm. Add a small seashell and a little seaweed to help contact the Great Sea of the collective unconscious. The crystal is rose quartz or turquoise. Tie in a *pale blue* cloth with rose-pink thread. A combination of mugwort, verbena and rose oils, or any single fragrance, will serve for the perfume oil.

Keep the charm at your workstation (say, in a desk drawer)

or in a pocket—as near to you as is practicable. Wear a dab of the oil at the base of the neck (check for skin sensitivity first)—somewhere you can smell it. Don't forget to 'cut' the pure essential oil with a carrier oil-sensitive skin can react badly to some of the pure oils.

Fast money spells and charms

Sometimes an unexpected expense crops up requiring urgent action, or a final demand notice drops into the letterbox. What you need is fast money, in fact.

If it's a full moon, you can follow the old English custom of going outside to greet the Lady as She rises, and turning the money in your pockets, while saying *Lady Moon, bring me silver to my need.* Or put all your silver coins in a silver dish with a piece of aventurine, and leave out in the moonlight for a moon bath. Use the same words. Of course, make sure that you leave dish and money in a safe place—or a passing pauper may think that the abundance is intended for them, not you!

Or you can go looking for a white horse, and when you find one, say:

White horse, white horse,
bring me good luck.
If I see a sovereign, let me pick it up.

This spell is very old—even older than the use of the sovereign, a gold coin which went out of circulation about a century ago, would suggest. It is in fact an invocation to the Celtic goddess Epona, whose symbol is the white horse. It might also be a useful spell for inveterate gamblers!

At new moon, when the first sliver of the new moon appears in the sky, try:

LOUISE HUEBNER'S FAST MONEY SPELL

✧ Stand outside your front door and throw brand-new coins into your house. Let them fall or roll where they will and don't pick them up for the rest of the month. The chant is 'money on the floor, money through the door'. Go to the trouble of getting mint-new coins from the bank, if you can.

The principle here is that:

(a) you are demonstrating that you trust in the universal abundance enough to throw money 'away', and
(b) like attracts like (new money attracts new money).

Brand-new coins will also (in theory, at least) be free of other people's vibes, so all the goodies will come your way. Since even 'mint-new' coins will have been handled by mint workers and the bank, the thinking seems a bit skewed. But if you're given new coins in change, you could set them to one side and when you have a fair handful, cleanse them by holding them under running water. And remember not to vacuum up the coins when you clean the house!

To attract money, Starhawk recommends a square of green cloth filled with borage, lavender, High John the Conqueror root, and saffron 'or any other appropriate herb', a few crystals of rock salt, and three silver coins. Tie it with gold and silver thread in eight knots. Do this on a Wednesday (Mercury's day), Thursday (Jupiter's day), or Sunday (the Sun's day) for best results.

Or you could try the West African spell quoted by Robin Skelton in *Spellcraft*:

Pay me a visit!
Pay me a visit!
O money, pay me a visit!
I'm living in this town!

WRITE A MAGIC CHEQUE SPELL

✦ Take your chequebook and write youself a cheque. Write your own name in the 'Pay To' line. If you need a specific amount to pay a bill, write that sum in the appropriate place. Otherwise leave it blank. In the space for your signature, write 'Law of Abundance'. Post the cheque to yourself, and wait.

Herbs (or spices) ruled by Jupiter are supposed to draw money and prosperity. You could try a pinch of cinnamon or nutmeg in your morning *caffe latte*. Or you may like to make:

JUPITER MONEY-DRAWING MIX

✦ Take a teaspoon (or thereabouts) each of:

- cinnamon
- cloves
- mustard seed
- nutmeg
- sandalwood
- tonka bean
- frankincense

- dried oak leaf
- hyssop
- sesame seeds

Grind in a mortar (on a Thursday, of course) until powdered. Put in a deep blue or gold pouch and carry on your person, or scatter it anywhere money is kept—purse, wallet or cash register.

All I can say about these is that they won't do any harm, and insofar as they encourage abundance-consciousness in you (i.e. you believe they will work), they may well draw money to you. The Jupiter mix will certainly make your purse and cash register smell interesting, and most of the ingredients could be added to a money-drawing curry (see Chapter Seven). By all means, try them.

I would, however, be more cautious about the following:

LOUISE HUEBNER'S LIFELONG MONEY INCREASE SPELL

This is to be worked at Spring Equinox. At one minute after midnight on the festival date, have set up:

- One gold candle—in the centre of the table
- Seven green candles—around the gold candle
- Nine white candles—around the green candles

Use salt to draw a circle round the circles of candles. Light the candles, then chant:

Orbiting Jupiter, trine the sun
Bring me money on the run.

❖ Finances should begin to improve within nineteen days.

It's an interesting concept, but when it's looked at more closely, may be an example of 'Be very careful what you ask for'.

The numerology and colours chosen suggest that this spell is based on Qabalah and the astrological associations of the sephiroth. I've analysed it accordingly.

The gold candle is clearly intended to represent gold, i.e. money—or possibly the Sun, which is fair enough since the Sun governs success, advancement and growth.

Then we have seven green candles. Seven is the number, and green the colour, attributed to the sephira *Netzach*, (Victory). So far, so good. But the planet associated with *Netzach* is Venus. What has Venus got to do with abundance, except as physical fertility? Fine if you're a farmer or a gardener. But if you are of childbearing age I'd suggest a degree of caution about lighting seven green candles. Or perhaps, given that Venus is the goddess of sexual love, it's suggesting that the best way to get fast money is in a horizontal position, as what's been called 'a lady of negotiable affection'.

Next we have a ring of nine white candles. Nine is the number and white (or silver) the colour associated with the sephira *Yesod*, the sphere of the moon. The negative aspect of *Yesod* is illusion or delusion. Is this whole thing a joke, a delusion? Are you working for the *illusion* of wealth?

And as for the circle of salt: it would keep snails at bay, but I don't think it would do much else, given that there is no stated purpose for its presence.

I have 'disassembled' this spell to show how important it is to *understand* what you're doing. If you don't understand all the elements of a spell or charm, then choose or devise something that you do understand.

Learning to distinguish between wants and needs

So—you have a satisfying job, you have money for food, bills, rent or mortgage, and some left over, for partying with your friends. You have what you need. But you want more—designer clothes, a new sports car, a beachside apartment. Yes, you can have them—if you work for them. You can do so magically, if you wish. If your will and ability to focus is sufficiently strong, nothing is impossible.

But begin to recognise that the more material things you want, the more you will continue to want. You are still not satisfying your basic need. The deprived baby is still crying out and reaching out, screaming 'Give me more . . . more . . . more!'

Abundance magic is most effective when it is used for need, not greed. If you work magic for what you need, the Universe will fulfill that need. For the rest, there's a price to pay. No, not your immortal soul—nothing can deprive you of that, though you can choose to starve it of nourishment. The price is one of time, energy, and perhaps friendship and family contact. Nothing is for nothing.

I am not suggesting that you narrow your horizons, or limit your capacity for enjoyment. You certainly should not buy into 'I don't deserve . . . I shouldn't expect . . .' Maybe for you, designer clothing is a need, not a want—if, for instance, you work in an industry where such things are part of your tools of trade. In any case, my idea of what I need will not be the same as yours, just as our wants, our 'wish list', will be different.

But I am suggesting that you look at what you think you want and ask if it will actually make you happy. Or is it simply a substitute for a need so basic that you're afraid even to name it—the need for unconditional love and acceptance?

Begin to think, not about what you want, but about what will—or even might—make you happy. Ask yourself what will give you joy. What is the feeling that I expect to have when I achieve . . . a holiday in Europe . . . a husband . . . a new car? Marion Weinstein, in her book *Positive Magic*, calls this making a distinction between *form* (the thing itself) and *essence* (what its real emotional significance is).

If you want that new DVD player because music gives you continuing joy and pleasure, and the DVD player, by providing better quality sound, will increase your pleasure, then working for the *form* (the DVD player itself) is entirely appropriate. If you want the player so that your brother will stop making cracks about outmoded technology (your old CD or, horrors, old cassette player) then the *essence* of what you want is for your brother's attitude to you to be accepting rather than critical. Simply working for the *form* of what you want will not satisfy your real need.

We have lots of wants that don't answer our needs. Relationships are probably the most pitfall-ridden area. You may say, or think, 'I want a husband'. What you may really mean is 'I want financial security'. (I know this may seem politically incorrect of me to say, but old conditioning rarely dies—it just goes underground.) Or perhaps you want emotional security. Or regular sex. Or someone to look after you and take out the rubbish bin.

Do you want a new job, or a pay rise? Or is your need really for more satisfying and fulfilling work, or for financial security—not having to worry about money? Then working for essence—for abundance, for fulfilment—may bring you a new job opportunity. Or you may find, or be shown, ways to make your present job fulfil your needs.

Even with apparently non-material wants, it's very useful to work to get below form to essence. It's a challenge, and requires a degree of self-knowledge, to get at the heart of your true need. For instance, 'I wish my sister (or mother, or boyfriend) would stop criticising me', may really mean 'I wish my sister would love and accept me for who I am.' This is the essence of what you want to happen.

If you work for essence, not form, the Universe will provide you with what you really need—which may well be greater or better than the thing or state you thought you wanted.

The Abundance Wish List: Spelling it Out

Get a notebook and start to list all the things that you believe would contribute to your happiness. Don't crowd them together—you'll need room to make notes. Give each wish its own page. By all means start off with the material things—a DVD player, a house with a view of the ocean or the mountains, a new car.

Now take a close look at them. Ask yourself, if this happened, how would I feel? The answer may not be what you were expecting.

The new car may be a status symbol—in which case, your need may be to feel important, an achiever, one of the high-flyers. There's nothing wrong with that. But in terms of the kind of abundance work I'm suggesting, it's important—imperative—that you recognise and work for your need. Otherwise you will waste time and energy on a series of wants, and be no closer to true abundance.

It may be that you want a new car because it provides a more reliable form of transport. Is this so you can reach that view of the ocean or the mountains? Why do you want the view? Because it makes you feel free? It lifts your spirits, inspires your work or your life? Is your real need a sense of openness and freedom? The new car may facilitate that, but it won't, in and of itself, provide it. The car is a means, not an end. There may be another, and even better, means to achieve that end.

As you begin to work on your wish list, you begin to realise that some—perhaps many—of the things you thought you wanted are really disguised needs.

Now ask yourself what you will have to do in order to bring the wish about. A new car is easy—research what make, what model will do what you want. Is fuel economy, ease of parking, efficient air conditioning or comfort on long drives your prime consideration? Some of them may be mutually exclusive, or require compromise—fuel economy and air conditioning, for instance. You may need to prioritise your requirements.

With non-material wishes, asking yourself what you need to do may require an uncomfortable degree of honesty. A better relationship with your mother or sibling may remove an irritation on which you've counted to give stability to your life. A husband, significant other or an intimate relationship will make demands on your free time and independence of action. You may need to let go of something—long-held resentment, picking up men (or women) in bars—in order to make space for what you really need.

Now look at your Abundance Wish List and begin to sort the items out into form and essence. Some decisions will be easy. You need a new toaster so you can make toast, or a breadmaker so you can bake your own bread. Clearly you're working for form—the thing itself. You're still thinking about whether a millionaire husband is form or essence. (A tip—it's definitely form!)

At last, it's time to start spellcasting. When you formulate each item on your Abundance Wish List, use the spell-model suggested by Marion Weinstein in *Positive Magic*. It's spellcrafting as positive affirmation. Believe me, this really works.

SPELLCRAFTING THE WEINSTEIN WAY

1. *There is One Power*

2. *And that Power is perfect abundance and fulfilment*

3. *And I* (your name) *am a perfect manifestation of that Power.*

4. *Therefore, perfect abundance and fulfilment are mine, here and now.*

5. *Specifically, by drawing into my life and my possession*

6. *The perfect* (car, house, CD) *which fulfils all my needs.*
For the good of all
And according to the free will of all
And so it must be.

Because we're really good at shooting ourselves in the foot, you may need or choose to add, after point 6, a point 7: *And I hereby release all negative causes, effects, manifestations, forms and the essence of worry which may hinder that fulfilment.*

If you want to work for essence—general abundance and fulfilment (the option I would recommend)—then omit points 5 and 6, but do add point 7. And always use the formula 'For the good of all; and according to the free will of all', thereby avoiding the Cosmic Wet Fish factor!

Once you've formulated your spell, you have a number of choices. You can write it out and put it around the house in places where your eyes are likely to fall—the hall or bathroom mirror, the fridge, the door of the cupboard where you keep the coffee. This is an especially good option if you've chosen to work for essence, since your abundance-consciousness is reinforced every time you see your spell.

If you're working for form—a specific item—the notes around the house may be counter-productive if they act as a reminder that the desired object is not yet in your possession. This is likely to reinforce poverty-consciousness. In that case, I would suggest:

WORKING FOR FORM

✦ Set up your dressing table or altar with one red candle (fire—representing your will) at your right hand, and a green candle (earth—representing steadfastness and earth-abundance) at your left hand. Write out your spell on good paper, in blue or green ink. Then read it aloud, as loudly and with as much conviction as you can muster. Now fold it in four, put the candles on the folded paper, and blow them out, saying:

The flame, but not the light.
As the light goes forth, so does my wish and my will,
So be it. So be it, So be it.

✦ Now don't touch candles or paper until your wish has come to pass. Then re-light the candles and burn the paper, giving thanks for a wish fulfilled. You can re-use the candles for further abundance work of this kind, but you shouldn't use them for other work.

As Marion Weinstein points out, you then need to 'act in accordance'—shop around, ask questions, generally open yourself to opportunity.

You can be specific and work for form, but do spend time, thought and effort in working out what you really and deeply *need.* Why work for form when you can work for essence? Work for 'the appropriate house' rather than 'a harbourside mansion' and see what delightful surprise the Universe has waiting for you.

And while you're building up those magical muscles, and working out the difference between wants and needs, try my all-singing, all-dancing, everything-but-the-kitchen-sink All-Purpose Abundance Charm.

ALL-PURPOSE ABUNDANCE CHARM

A personal favourite. One of these lives alongside my computer. It would also make a good *potpourri* to attract abundance to your home or office. In that case put it in a pretty bowl—there are some with openwork lids especially for *potpourri*.

✧ You will need:

- a square of purple cloth (of reasonable size)
- gold and silver-coloured embroidery silk
- bay leaf, St John's Wort, cassia, frankincense—ruled by the Sun
- mugwort, camomile—ruled by the Moon, for intuition
- lavender, bergamot, fennelseed—ruled by Mercury, for ease of communication
- allspice, coriander, oakmoss—under Mars, for strength, courage and vitality

- rose petals—under Venus, for love, charm and good partying
- nutmeg, clove, sandalwood—ruled by Jupiter, for abundance-consciousness
- some grain—rice, wheat, corn, oats—for the Element of Earth
- some seaweed or a seashell—for the Element of Water
- a birdseye chili—for the Element of Fire
- a small feather—for the Element of Air
- a gold and a silver coin—e.g. a dollar, a ten cent piece—to attract money
- sugar for sweetness, salt for savour, sesame for opening doors
- small tumbled pieces of rose quartz, aventurine (the Gambler's Stone), clear quartz, carnelian and lapis lazuli.

✦ Place all, or as many of the above as you have conveniently to hand—but at least one per planet and element—into the cloth. Tie, pudding-style, with gold and silver embroidery silk, using four knots in each. Hold the charm in your hands, kneading it and smelling its fragrance, as you chant:

By the power of three times three
Bring abundance here to me!

✦ This should be said nine times.

✦ An abundance charm of this kind should be put together during a new or waxing moon, and during the waxing half of the year—winter solstice to summer solstice. The perfect time would be at waxing or full moon, on the Vernal (Spring) Equinox.

Abundance amulets and talismans

After all I've just been saying about abundance-consciousness, going to the trouble of making an amulet or talisman seems rather beside the point. The power is in you, in your imagination and your will, not in any thing. Besides, if you can afford to have an abundance amulet made, then you probably don't need to wear one. However . . .

- An **amulet** of Jupiter should be made of pure tin, as a setting for a ring or pendant of lapis lazuli or a cabochon-cut sapphire. On the lapis lazuli should be engraved the astrological symbol for Jupiter, together with the Zodiac sign of your birth, and your initials, pointed (picked out) with gold leaf or gold dust. If you are using a sapphire, these symbols may be engraved on the tin which backs the setting. Such an amulet should be consecrated and charged on a Thursday, under the auspices of the archangel Tzadkiel.

- A **talisman** of Jupiter is also to be engraved on pure tin (Jupiter's metal), using the symbols specified above. It should be wrapped in purple silk after being consecrated and charged. This is the simplest form of abundance talisman—there are much more complex and complicated ones. (See the Skelton or Gonzalez-Wippler books listed in Sources and Further Reading for details and illustrations.)

There are, of course, simple 'lucky pieces' which, since most people consider luck and money to be interchangeable, are in effect abundance amulets. These include:

Common 'good luck' tokens

- the lucky rabbit's foot (not so lucky for the rabbit, of course)
- the shamrock
- the horse-shoe—often nailed over a front door, to bring luck to the house and its inhabitants. Remember to place it points up, 'to keep the luck from running away'. This is old Celtic magic—the horse is the symbol of Epona.
- the Cornish piskie (no, I don't mean pixie) sometimes called Joan the Wad
- a gold sovereign set as a ring, or a number of them in a necklace—a way of carrying your good fortune with you as a negotiable asset (Gypsy magic)
- an amber necklace or a large piece of amber—the electrostatic charge amber carries when rubbed with silk is believed to 'attract' good luck
- a palm-size touchstone of aventurine, the 'Gambler's Stone'
- the *t'ai chi t'u* (yin/yang) symbol—also a symbol of balance
- an image of Ganesha, the Hindu god of good luck
- the Hebrew letter *Shin*
- a miniature rake (for raking in good luck—a *feng shui* symbol)

- a miniature cauldron—a Celtic good luck charm—the symbol of abundance, of good cheer and good company
- the triple spiral (as carved on the lintel at Newgrange in Ireland)—abundance as the gift of the Triple Goddess
- any token that you think, believe or hope brings you good luck.

And the best of luck to you!

Chapter Six

things that go bump in the night: psychic protection and self-defence

'Just because you're paranoid doesn't mean you're not being followed.'
Colin Vancao

So you've read a couple of books about magic, or you've joined a psychic development course or a meditation group—and suddenly your nights are filled with dreams from which you wake sweating, pursued by nameless horrors. Are you under psychic attack?

The answer, in all probability, is a resounding NO.

Have you been doing anything likely to attract unwelcome

attention, like barging in with candles, incense and holy water to exorcise someone's reputedly haunted house? Do you really have sufficient magical oomph to represent a serious threat to someone with a fragile grasp on their sense of self-esteem *and* the ability and desire to send some nastiness your way?

Basically, are you *important* enough to warrant the effort and energy involved in true psychic attack?

Generally speaking, black magicians (a rarer breed than many people think) are too busy trying to take over the world (or possibly the Universe) to concern themselves with you. Or me, for that matter.

Psychic attack does happen—*malocchio, sematiaxe, sihir* are all words for 'giving the eye' (the evil eye, hexing, illwishing) to someone who is disliked, envied or resented. Thoughts and words have power (this is, after all, the basis of spellcraft), and malice is a powerful emotion to drive the hex home.

But before you start investing in a shop full of protective amulets or flee to your parish priest in search of exorcism, there are some useful questions to ask yourself.

First, look for a physical cause. A hot night and too many bedclothes, choosing toasted cheese or sardine sandwiches for a late-night snack, watching a horror movie on the TV—any of these may give you a bad night's sleep.

Next, has someone told you, or hinted, that 'someone' has hexed you? For illwishing to work the recipient has to find out or be told that the curse has been placed; and they have to believe in the possibility of such a thing. Then the imagination goes into action. If you begin to believe you're unlucky, the Universe will oblige by providing you with more examples of your bad luck. Remember, like attracts like.

Now, check the phase of the moon. Full moon and dark moon (the pause between waning and waxing phases of the moon) tend to be psychically turbulent. The more that magic sharpens your perceptions, the more you are likely to be affected by the phase of the Moon. Dreams will be more vivid, and restful sleep harder to achieve. It's the astral equivalent to being caught in cross-currents while swimming.

The phase of the moon can certainly affect both sleep and behaviour patterns. I used to swim at a pool where one of the other regulars worked the night shift at a residential care unit for developmentally delayed adults. Some mornings, he'd come in looking particularly worn out. Rough night? Yes, everyone had been restless and one or two clients had become abusive and/or violent. Of course, it had been a full moon. (This was his own observation, unprompted by me.)

But sometimes there was no full moon to account for the disturbed behaviour. We worked out that these episodes had in fact occurred at dark of the moon. It seems to be that change of phase, like the change of a tide, affects those open to the moon's influence. Given that the human body is made up of something like nine-tenths water, and the moon governs the tides, this is hardly surprising.

The term 'lunatic' itself comes from the idea that Luna (Latin for the Moon and the Goddess who rules it) can drive men mad. Police officers also confirm that 'fruitloops and nutters' (in their politically incorrect but colourful parlance) tend to be thicker on the ground at full moon.

So there are all kinds of restless and disturbed vibes out there. It's hardly surprising that you may be starting to pick them up.

As you grow in magic, you may find that you have a capacity and calling to work for and with the lost and troubled at such times. I *strongly* recommend, however, that you don't rush into this area without proper training and support. It is work best and safest done in a group, where there are people trained to watch your back and get you out of trouble if necessary.

In the meantime, it's a good idea to **put up wards** before going to sleep on full or dark moon nights. In fact, setting up protection for yourself (and your family) before sleep every night is a good habit to get into. It will tend to ensure peaceful sleep no matter what the moon phase.

Putting up wards

To 'ward' is to guard—the words are from the same source. When you put up or set up wards, you are setting up a kind of astral barrier or wall—in a way similar to that of a magical circle cast before beginning ritual work.

In the beginning it's useful to devise and use a form of words—a spell—combined with visualisation, to set up your wards. The spoken word, as we've already established, carries its own power. Later, once the wards are well established, it may be sufficient to visualise the wards (usually in the form of pentagrams) clicking into place.

So: what words, what visualisations?

ST PATRICK'S BREASTPLATE

✥ You may choose to use the cardinal archangels, Raphael, Michael, Gabriel and Uriel, perhaps in the form known as 'St Patrick's Breastplate'.

✥ Face east and say:

Before me Raphael
(visualise a bright yellow pentagram flaming at East)
Behind me Gabriel
(visualise a vibrant blue pentagram flaming at West)
To my right hand, Michael
(visualise a bright red pentagram flaming at South)
To my left hand, Uriel.
(visualise a deep green pentagram flaming at North)
Around me flame the pentagrams

(hold the visualisation of all four pentagrams)
Above me burns the six-rayed star.
(visualise a six-pointed star of deep amethyst over your head, with the rays cascading around you in a fountain of light)
Against such warding, no evil shall prevail.

St Patrick's Breastplate is designed to give you personal protection. If you wish to extend it to all inhabitants in your house, you need to extend the pentagrams beyond your personal aura (which extends, roughly speaking, an arm's length all around your body). Visualise the pentagrams at the outer walls of the house, or at the borders of the property.

You can of course go further and visualise great winged Beings of might and power standing at each Quarter, but it smacks of overkill when all you want is a good night's sleep. I invoke the Archangels when the ritual work in hand requires the astral equivalent of a full suit of body armour rather than a padded jacket. It's not that they object to being asked for help—their will is to wait on the will of the Most High—but it's a bit like appealing to the Supreme Court over a parking fine.

However, angels, archangels and all the company of Heaven may not be your scene. You may think of angels as wishy-washy figures wearing white night-shirts and a sickly-sweet smile. If this is the case, calling on the Archangels for help is going to be about as useful as calling on the Easter Bunny. You will need to find a form or archetype that has protective power for you. In the Celtic tradition we call on the elemental Powers.

CELTIC WARDING

✥ If you use this method, turn to face each Quarter (direction) as you speak, and visualise or draw the pentagram (or the Celtic cross if you prefer) in the appropriate colour. Say:

✥ At East:
Guardians of the Watchtowers and Gateways of the East,
Powers of Air:
Circle and protect me, and help me in the work of this night.
Be welcome (draw a yellow pentagram). *I am blessed*
by your presence.

✥ At South:
Guardians of the Watchtowers and Gateways of the South,
Powers of Fire:
Circle and protect me, and help me in the work of this night.
Be welcome (draw a red pentagram). *I am blessed*
by your presence.

✥ At West:
Guardians of the Watchtowers and Gateways of the West,
Powers of Water:
Circle and protect me, and help me in the work of this night.
Be welcome (draw a blue pentagram). *I am blessed*
by your presence.

✥ At North:
Guardians of the Watchtowers and Gateways of the North,
Powers of Earth:
Circle and protect me, and help me in the work of this night.

Be welcome (draw a green pentagram). *I am blessed by your presence.*

✦ When all four pentagrams are burning brightly (it can take a while to get the knack of holding the visualisations in all four directions, but I assure you, it can be done!), call in the fifth element of Spirit and say:

Powers above and Powers below, Powers without and Powers within,
Circle and protect me, guide, guard, heal and hallow me
And bring me safe home. I give you my thanks and my blessing.

You will observe that the place of the Power of Spirit is at the centre, the heart of the circle. It is your ground of being—the place where you are. You are now enclosed and enfolded in a sphere of rainbow light.

The phrase 'Guardians of the Watchtowers' is almost certainly a borrowing from ceremonial magic, but is widely used in Wiccan (Gardnerian and Alexandrian) rites. It has a nice ring to it, but if it bothers you, find a phrase that doesn't. Just make sure that it has the same kind of ring and rhythm. Somehow 'Hey guys, now listen up!' doesn't quite do it for me.

You will also find southern hemisphere pagans who insist that Fire should be at North and Earth at South. I know the arguments, but I choose to work Northern, since that is the home of my tradition. However, if you personally find/think/feel that working Southern is right for you, the choice is yours to make. Just remember that your circle will have to be cast *widdershins* (anti-clockwise) in order for the elements to follow the correct (air-fire-water-earth) sequence.

Why is that the 'correct' sequence? You will find various

reasons given for working *deosil* or *widdershins* (clockwise or anticlockwise), including the movement of the Sun and the way water goes down the plug-hole in your bath. It's actually much simpler than that. Most earth-magic is designed to bring the thing or state desired into physical manifestation—into the 'real world'. So the energy moves from the most refined or ethereal (air) to the most dense (earth). Spirit both begins and completes the process.

Widdershins (counterclockwise) has a bad press in magical work—it's considered to be the direction of negative or black magic. In Northern work this means that it moves 'against the Sun', from manifest to unmanifest, from life to not-life. There are times when this movement of energy is entirely appropriate—for example, if you are doing release work for an earthbound soul. But these are high and weighty matters, not to be undertaken lightly or unadvisedly. Unless you're working Southern, it's as well to avoid working widdershins.

Drawing the pentagram

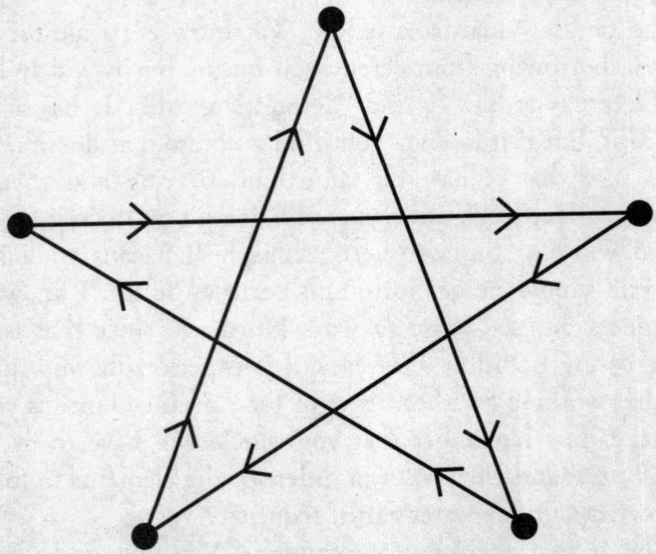

This is much more easily demonstrated than described. The pentagram is a five-pointed star with one point (representing Spirit) uppermost. There are various ways of drawing it, but the most common is top point to bottom left, to upper right, across to upper left, down to lower right, and up again to the top.

The thing to remember is not to be timid. If you're drawing a pentagram, do it with the full sweep of your outstretched arm. Confidence in its efficacy is a large part of the magic. A cautiously outstretched finger is not going to convey to the Powers that you believe in either them or yourself.

Drawing the Celtic Cross

The Celtic Cross, or the Cross of the Elements, is an equal-armed cross within a circle. In protective work it is drawn top to bottom (North to South), left to right (West to East). From East a circle is drawn deosil (clockwise) connecting the four points of the compass and ending again at East.

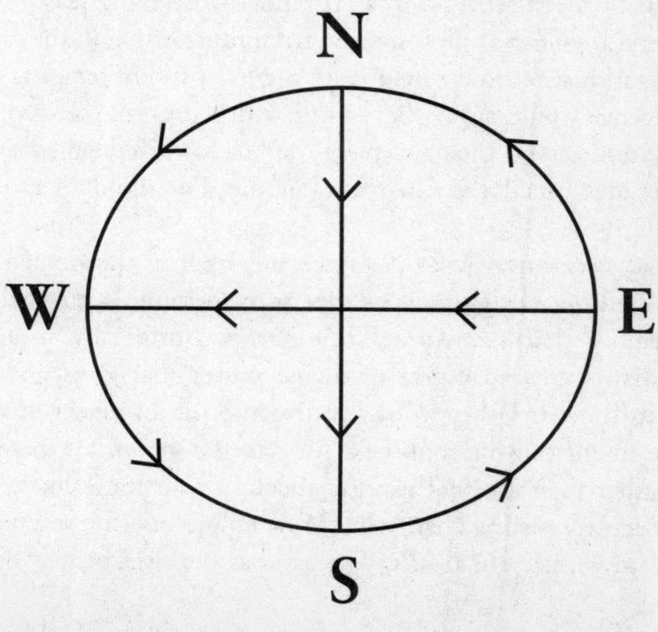

So you've tried some or all of the exercises suggested, and the nightmares and sense of foreboding remain, or increase. What's going on? Is it a sign from God that your interest in matters magical is sinful, evil, wicked—or just dangerous to your sanity?

Are you (perhaps unconsciously) *expecting* to be attacked? Old conditioning goes very deep. You may have been brought up—as many are—to believe that, for example, Tarot cards are the Devil's Picture Book, and meddling with such things is a sure path to damnation. As an adult you have rightly rejected this as nonsense. But child-self remembers, and remembers stories of wicked witches and black shadows lurking in the wardrobe. And so the boogieman walks in your dreams.

Maybe it's your daylight life that's been thrown into turmoil. Arguments with workmates, threats from your boss, difficulties with your family (or, even more threatening, with your partner)—you feel that the world has become an unfriendly place. It's only a small step from that to 'somebody's doing this to me . . . somebody is illwishing me . . . *they* are out to get me.'

Taken to extremes, this is paranoia—or at the least, acute anxiety. If your fear prevents you from functioning in the everyday world, seek expert help from a good psychotherapist. (My preference would always be for one with a Jungian background. They understand the concept of the Shadow, the denied self—sometimes called the Guardian on the Threshold in esoteric writing.)

And very often what is presenting itself is the denied self projected outwards—your own personal demon. It may help to remember that the word, spelt *daemon*, originally meant a guardian spirit, an aspect of divine power that gives good or bad fortune. In other words, your demon is an aspect of what some might call the soul, or a Jungian the *animus* or *anima*.

Rather than external psychic attack, it's far more likely that your ego is resisting change by throwing up long-forgotten fears to stop you in your tracks. The ego has the firm belief: 'If you change, I die'. It will do anything to push you back inside its comfort zone.

But knowing in your head (or hearing it from someone like me) that your fears are not logical, or grounded in reality, doesn't necessarily make the night terrors go away. What will help most is taking some action.

That action may not be what you think of as magical. Spells and charms are not the answer to every problem.

Spells and charms are not the answer to every problem.

A good laugh is a great cure for heaviness of spirit. Go to a comedy with a friend or get a funny video out. Settle down and spend an evening with something (or someone) self-indulgent and probably involving chocolate. Do this as a conscious act of 'yah boo, rack off hairylegs' to the glooms, and watch them vanish, or at least assume their proper proportion.

It may also be appropriate at this stage to speak to a counsellor or take a personal growth course. You may simply need insight into the baggage you've been carrying, which the ego doesn't want you to acknowledge and release. If you can track down a course or counsellor working with a process called *psychosynthesis*, you may well find it answers your need.

And there's nothing that says you shouldn't devise a spell or light a candle to guide you to the right course, or the right counsellor!

TO ASK FOR GUIDANCE

✦ Light a yellow candle and say: *Powers of Air, guide me to the right person or course to ease my troubled mind.*

✦ Light a red candle and say: *Powers of Fire, give me the courage and will to pursue my chosen path.*

✦ Light a blue candle and say: *Powers of Water, soothe my troubled heart and wash away all tears and fears from me. Help me be open to my ability to flow and change.*

✦ Light a green candle and say: *Powers of Earth, uphold and sustain me, give me steadfastness in my quest for self-knowledge.*

✦ Light a white or violet candle and say: *Power of Spirit, I place my trust in you and in my own inner knowing to bring me to safe harbour.*

✦ Draw the power of each element into your aura, and say: *Fiat, fiat, fiat—so be it.*

If it's possible to do so safely, leave the candles to burn out—a good reason for getting a supply of small (votive) candles in a range of colours (see Chapter Three). If this isn't possible, light the candles for (say) ten to thirty minutes every day, depending on how long you have available to sit with them. Repeat until they are burnt out.

But perhaps it's not you, but a beloved child that is waking with the night terrors. If you're becoming more sensitive, so perhaps are they—psychic sensitivity often runs in families. It's possible to help them without the sort of fuss that's going to have them taking a pentacle to Show and Tell.

If the child is quite young, a nightlight (electrical rather than a candle) will often suffice. If it is in the shape or has a picture of one of the traditional guardians of children (a bear, for instance) and the child is told that the animal is there to frighten off anything nasty or scary, so much the better.

Older children can be given a simple form of words with which to claim their own space. My husband's godson, then aged about nine, was sleeping badly and having nightmares. Ray went in to him after he'd gone to bed, and told him to point into each corner of his bedroom and say 'This is my room. Go away. You don't belong here'. It worked, and has continued to do so—the family has since moved house, the nine-year-old is now twenty, and his bedroom in the new house still has wards in the corner of each room—wards he doesn't remember consciously setting.

Basic psychic hygiene: aura and chakra cleansing

All of us at some time have to go into places or mix with people that/who 'feel' wrong—whether you call it negative vibes or an unhealthy atmosphere. We ride public transport, go to shopping centres, maybe go to a party at which one particular person gives us the creeps. What can be done to offset the negative influences?

First, it may be possible simply to leave. It's all right to claim a headache, because if you stay there you'll probably end up with one. No need to create a fuss—just excuse yourself and go. But you may be at a dinner party or an office function where it's not polite or politic to leave. You may have to go to the shopping mall (they're generally worse than High Street shopping strips, or even supermarkets) to pay bills. And you need to use public transport to get to work.

One of the simplest ways of dealing with shopping mall and public transport greeblies is a dab of **pure sandalwood oil** on the nape of the neck. This permeates the aura and strengthens the auric field (don't ask me how—it just works!) making it difficult for negative energies to latch on to you.

Surrounding yourself with a **golden egg** (with a nice, hard shell) is the favourite of a friend of mine. Again, what this does is strengthen the auric field to make it impermeable to nasties. The 'shell' of the egg coincides with the periphery of the aura—stretch both arms out at your sides to get a general idea of its extent.

I use and recommend the **Suit of Lights**. Imagine the astral equivalent of an all-in-one catsuit or diver's wetsuit. It covers the whole body (including hands and feet) except for a small area of the face (the oval of eyes/nose/mouth). If it helps visualisation, imagine putting it on a piece at a time, as one does a wetsuit. The Suit of Lights is made up of thousands of tiny reflective mirrors. Its function is to bounce back to the sender any negativity directed at you. It's particularly useful if you are going into a place or situation, which you know beforehand, is likely to be difficult.

Mirror magic generally is a useful and simple way of bouncing back negative energies—a *feng shui* mirror works on this principle. But a hand or purse mirror will do just as well. Hold it between your hands and say *I charge this mirror to deflect all negative energies from this place.* If you have a sense that the negativity is coming from a particular direction, place the mirror on a windowsill facing that direction. If your sleep is troubled, put it on your bedroom windowsill. It's especially useful as an adjunct to formal warding at full and dark moons.

These are all preventative measures. What do you do if you find that you've already unwittingly picked up the auric equivalent of dogshit on your shoe?

First, and most practically, take a shower. In this case, cleanliness really is next to godliness. Wash yourself thoroughly, including your hair. Have ready a jug or bowl containing salt, vinegar (cider is good and will also give your hair a gloss) and water. When you've finished washing, pour the contents of the jug over your head and visualise the water sluicing away any remaining auric sludge. It's OK to rinse the mixture off under the shower—it has done its work.

AURIC RINSE

- 1 tablespoon of rock or sea salt
- 20 ml of cider vinegar
- 1 litre of water
- 2 drops pure sandalwood oil
- 2 drops pure hyssop oil (if obtainable)

❖ Combine and use as a rinse after your shower. If you like, you can make up a quantity of the salt/vinegar/sandalwood mix and have it standing by.

Or you can make up an aromatic herbal aura cleanser:

CASS' MAGIC AURA CLEANSER

❖ Take equal quantities of hyssop, rosemary, lavender, oakmoss, mugwort and basil. Put into spring water, bring to the boil, and simmer for half an hour (you are technically making a decoction). Leave to stand awhile, then strain (your compost heap will like the herbs). Add sea or rock salt, and cider vinegar. Stir in and allow to cool. Add oils of sandalwood, frankincense, pine, bergamot and vervain—a few drops of each. Put into a suitable bottle (plastic is fine if you're going to be keeping it in the bathroom; glass in the foot is not a good look!). Put a little in a bowl or jug and top up with water. Use as a rinse after your shower, or (if you're feeling really grimy) put some in your bath for a long soak (but remember to dunk your hair!).

✧ You can if you wish add bicarbonate of soda to the decoction. It will make your skin feel smooth, and is another traditional aura cleanser—but it will make the decoction foam up, especially if added while it's still hot. Take the pot off the stove and allow to cool unless you want a major clean-up job on your hands.

Needless to say, these are for external use only, but one friend who took a daring sip (I would advise you not to do this) of my herbal decoction said it really didn't taste too bad, and the effect on his bowels was, well, extraordinarily cleansing!

As with any of these recipes, if you don't have or can't get some of the ingredients, it's all right to improvise—for example, using aromatherapy oils instead of herbs. Only the hyssop, sandalwood oil, salt and vinegar are absolutely essential. The other herbs and oils bring in various protective and clarifying energies which give some added oomph to the formulation. If you're going to use oils, take the trouble (and extra expense) to get pure essential oils, not synthetics.

So your aura is so clean it squeaks. How do you keep it that way? The Fountain Exercise is very effective and daily use is recommended.

THE FOUNTAIN EXERCISE

✦ Imagine that under your feet is a fountain of sparkling energy coming from deep in the earth. It surges up, through your body, to a point about a foot above your head. There it cascades out and down as a fountain of iridescent white light, following the egg shape of the auric shell, until it returns to the earth.

✦ Any negative energy is washed out of the aura, removed and recycled into the earth. The fountain surges up again, and again, until you feel cleansed and revitalised. Use for some minutes morning and evening, or as needed.

The Fountain Exercise has a venerable heritage, going back to the Order of the Golden Dawn and beyond. I learnt it from training papers issued by the Servants of the Light (for contact details, see Suppliers and Resources at the end of the book), where it is one of the earliest meditation exercises a student tackles. Israel Regardie, in *The Art of True Healing*, says: 'No single atom or cell in any organ or limb is omitted from the influence of its healing, regenerative power.'

The great advantage of the Fountain Exercise is its discretion. It can be used or practised anywhere—at your desk, on the train, in the supermarket—places where reciting St Patrick's Breastplate, drawing pentagrams in the air, or taking a shower may be neither possible nor appropriate.

It can also be used, quite effectively, to cleanse a place that gives you the heebie-jeebies. It's not an exorcism—that requires special skills and training, and if you find yourself in such a place, call in the experts (see 'Consulting an Expert', below). It's more like a kind of psychic/astral vacuum cleaner—it will remove surface dust and grime, but it won't shampoo the carpets or scrub down the walls.

However, it's definitely better than doing nothing, and may—for example, in a hospital emergency room—do a lot of good. There are places, like hospitals and funeral chapels, where negative energies—pain, fear, grief—pile up and nobody thinks (or knows how) to do anything about them. The Fountain Exercise is something you can do to help.

THE RING-PASS-NOT

This visualisation was a particular favourite of Dion Fortune's. It's tricky to get the hang of, but useful because it's virtually instantaneous.

- Visualise a wide band of light spinning clockwise around you at a distance roughly that of your outstretched arms.

- Then visualise a second band within the first *spinning in the opposite direction.*

- Extend those bands over your head and under your feet so that each becomes a spinning sphere.

- Hold the visualisation for as long as you can. (You can be pretty pleased with yourself if you manage to achieve the visualisation *at all* the first time you try it!)

The idea behind the Ring-Pass-Not and the reason for its name is that any entity that manages to penetrate the first ring (by synchronising with its spinning speed) will then bounce off the second ring, which is hurtling in the opposite direction. This will either send the entity (or energy bundle) spinning into the distant regions of astral space with the equivalent of a splitting headache, or cause it to disintegrate in the space between the two rings. Neat, huh?

Using sound for psychic protection

An actor friend tells the story of working in a provincial theatre which was reputed to be haunted. One night he and his girlfriend had to work back to finish some sets and costumes for the next production. After they'd finished they went back to the upstairs dressing room to collect their belongings. As they walked along the corridor, they became aware of a sudden and considerable drop in temperature and had the sensation of being watched by some presence both malevolent and hungry. The girlfriend screamed, a darkness gathered at the end of the corridor—and Colin took a pistol loaded with blanks, a prop for the production, and fired six shots into the darkness. The theatre remained untroubled by its ghost as long as he was working there.

This may not be the best and most compassionate way to deal with lost souls (see the section on release work below) but it was certainly effective. Presumably the sharp and repeated report of the blanks changed the vibratory rate of the 'haunted' area. Or maybe it just said 'I'm not scared of you. Rack off, hairylegs!' I don't specially recommend it as a technique, but as an example of how sound can be used to 'clear' a space.

Similarly, **drumming** is an effective way of creating sacred space (as in Native American rituals). It can also be used to clear someone's aura before or as part of healing work, and is a vital part of shamanic journeying.

In Eastern spiritual practice—e.g. Tibetan Buddhism—

chanting is used. It has a number of functions, but cleansing and preparing sacred space is certainly important. In the West, Gregorian chant serves a similar function—although I know a number of people who dislike Gregorian chant because they associate it with early and unfortunate experience of Christianity. If you don't like Gregorian because of its patriarchal associations, look out for the music of Hildegarde of Bingen (*Voice of the Blood, Heavenly Revelations, Songs of Ecstasy*—all on CD), which may be more to your taste.

Sound is a quick and simple way to change the 'vibes' of a place or to lift a depressed mood. It is useful to have a selection of music geared to soothe or enliven at need. More specifically, put some effort into finding a piece of music that calms and uplifts you (Bach's *Jesu Joy of Man's Desiring* is one that works for me). Use it as part of your warding and cleansing work. In time—usually quite a short time—it will become associated in your mind with the wards, and playing it—or even humming a few bars in a tight spot—will cause the wards to click into place. Gives a new meaning to 'Whistle a happy tune', doesn't it?

Chakra cleansing, energy junkies and psychic vampirism

Chakras are vortices (whirlpools) of energy located in the aura but connected to the physical body, which they energise in various ways. The word chakra comes from Sanskrit and means 'wheel'. This is a specialist and complex subject, and I refer you to the reading list for more exhaustive discussion of each chakra, its location and function. Suffice it to say that they are a very important part of the body's subtle anatomy, and dysfunction in a chakra can and probably will affect some aspect of your physical, emotional or mental well-being.

From the point of view of psychic protection and self-defence, you need to be aware that energy can be drained from you through one or more chakras. This doesn't have to be a conscious act on the part of the person doing the draining, so in that sense it is not an act of malice.

We've all known people who seem to go out of their way to seek our company, and by subtle flattery and little presents make us feel valued—at the time. After a while you notice that after a couple of hours with them, you come away feeling exhausted. But they're so nice, so kind-hearted ... and they really value you, ask for your advice, appreciate the time you spend with them ... So the next time they suggest meeting up, along you go. And once again, you end up feeling exhausted.

This exhaustion is quite different from the 'I've been out and had a really good time, but now I need to sleep' tiredness. You don't feel pleasantly weary. You feel washed out. Listless. As though there's a dirty grey curtain between you and the sun.

Unless you're coming down with the flu, you've attracted an energy junkie into your environment.

Once you begin to suspect what's happening, you will start to notice that as you get more tired, they get livelier and more energetic. They leave your company feeling on top of the world. Naturally, they want to maintain the contact.

I would like to stress that generally this energy draining is quite unconscious—if it were conscious, it would count as a very nasty piece of negative magic. If the energy draining is conscious you're dealing with someone who is more accurately called a psychic vampire (except that, unlike the vampires of fiction, they don't automatically transform you into a vampire as well).

So what do you do?

You may choose to let the situation continue, and use the Fountain exercise to increase your available energy. This may be appropriate if you feel that the person really needs *and is entitled* to call on your energy—for instance, they may be seriously ill or passing through an emotional crisis. Your partner, your child, your parent may fall into this category. If you are giving informed consent and can find ways to compensate for the energy loss (meditation, taking time out for yourself) this may be an acceptable, though it should really be only a short-term solution. Ideally you should learn to draw energy from the earth or the Universe rather than deplete your personal energy field.

You can of course just stop socialising with the energy junkie, but this may be at least embarrassing, and if the person is a relative (your mother-in-law or sister, for instance) simply not practicable.

Or you can undertake the more difficult and challenging task of detaching the hooks and energy lines they've lodged in one or more of your chakras, and sealing the aura so it won't happen again.

The chakras most commonly affected by this sort of activity are the solar plexus (an input point for physical vitality, the *chi* or *elan vital*) and the belly chakra (emotional energy and stability). Hooks into the heart chakra do occur, but are usually the result of a close and affectionate bond (mother to child, lover to lover) and are less problematic. However, if you have been in an intimate relationship with someone, you've broken up but still feel connected and unable to move on, you may need to unhook a cord into the heart chakra (see Chapter Four). Hooks into the other chakras are relatively less common.

WHAT IS A CHAKRA HOOK AND WHAT CAN I DO ABOUT IT?

Imagine a fish-hook, with a line or cord attached and leading back to the person utilising your energy. The energy pulses or travels along the cord from you to him or her—never in the opposite direction. You need to visualise unhooking the connection and sending it back to where it belongs—with love and light, if possible, rather than animosity. Remember, the person doing this doesn't usually realise what they're doing, so anger isn't appropriate and will make the disconnection more difficult. If it helps the visualisation, imagine that the cord is a piece of overstretched elastic. Once you unhook it, it will twang back to its proper place.

Some chakra hooks and cords can go back to a previous life. I was told of one case in which a couple had worked magically together in this and at least one previous life. The man died, and it seemed likely that his partner would follow him, although she was still a relatively young woman. Her spiritual teacher told her she still had much to do and offer in this life, and helped her release a hook about the size of a harpoon, and a cord which was so thick that she said it was like hacking through a ship's hawser.

Most hooks and cords are fish-hook and string size. If you find yourself with something suitable for catching a fighting marlin, seek expert help. You may need to do the release work in a ritual context, properly protected.

Once the hook and cord are released, you need to repair the rent made in the chakra by the hook. Simply see the rip or tear closing over, as good as new. Or visualise yourself sewing the tear together with your best and finest stitches (good for embroiderers and plastic surgeons!). If you're of a medical turn of mind, the little plastic strips (Steristrips, butterfly sutures) now used instead of catgut stitches may be the way to go. Astral Superglue has been suggested, not entirely in jest. Whatever image works for you is the one to use.

Once you've done the work of detaching the cord, you will probably find that the person who's been drawing energy from you ceases to be quite so fond of your company. They may actually complain that you're not as much fun as you used to be . . . even that you've become dull and boring. If you've talked to them at all about matters magical and/or spiritual, your new interests may well be blamed for the change in you. And, of course, they're quite right. You've learned how to protect yourself against being used to kick-start somebody else's life. Who knows, eventually they may learn to become energetically self-sufficient.

OPENING AND CLOSING DOWN THE CHAKRAS

There are exercises and visualisations for opening and closing the chakras at will. I suggest caution unless you are being supervised by a teacher whose experience and ethics you trust. Ideally they will also have the clairvoyant ability to 'see' what's going on. Otherwise, it's an area where fools rushing in may find themselves on an unpleasantly steep learning curve.

Of dragons and other guardians

Remember that imaginary playmate you had as a small child? The one you could share your troubles with, who was there for you when life was tough and the nights were dark? You can use your imagination—the most powerful tool of magic—to create and empower an astral guardian to assist and protect you in everyday life (and also in your magical work, but that's another and more complex story).

In shamanic work such a guardian is known as your power animal, and can take many shapes—wolf, bear or snake, for example. Power animals are individual—specific, and tend to find (or choose) you rather than the other way round. Discovering your power animal and establishing a *rapport* takes time and training. (Workshops that promise to make you a shamanic elder in a single weekend are both silly and potentially dangerous.)

Dragons, however, tend to be much more accessible.

Stop thinking of dragons as nasty, scaly creatures given to eating maidens out of season. They are creatures of great magical power, astral embodiments of earth-energy who are more than capable of protecting you, your car, your house—even your luggage.

Some years ago I was travelling from Penzance to Exeter in the south-west of Britain and got chatting to Morwenna, who at 17 was embarked on the great adventure of going up to London to study art and design. We'd been talking about herbs and healing, and she was clearly open-minded to the concept of alternative realities. After a while she admitted she was nervous about living in London. She'd heard stories about unpleasant types coming up to someone with a backpack, slitting it open with a knife, and making off with the contents.

I suggested she park a small dragon on her backpack with instructions to see off unwelcome attention. Er . . . how would she do that? I asked what colour her backpack was. It's a sort of lolly-pink. Right. A small purple dragon with a lime-green underbelly would colour-coordinate nicely. He'd have to curl around the backpack, so we'd better give him claws to hang on with—and, of course to warn off a potential malefactor. Emerald green would look good. Now, she should close her eyes and see him clearly curled round her backpack (which was in the luggage section some feet away).

After a few moments she opened her eyes wide in surprise. 'I can see him! He winked at me! He's got long eyelashes!' Good! Now go back and ask him his name. But don't tell me, or anyone else, OK? She did, and the answer clearly amused her. By this time we were pulling into Exeter station, and I made my farewells and left. But somewhere in Britain there's a young Cornishwoman who knows that Dragon Power Rules, OK! I hope Morwenna still has her dragon. As long as she remembers him (and his name), he will be around.

Several of my friends have car-dragons whose job is to protect the car from theft and accident, and sometimes find a parking space. Their hard work should however be acknowledged. Hilary throws her dragon an astral chicken (uncooked—a dragon can flame its own dinner) every so often. Lyn's dragon is partial to marshmallows and lamingtons.

Another friend always says 'Tails!' before closing the boot of his car as a reminder to the dragons to keep their tails out of what Americans call a tailgate. On one occasion he and a friend were in a pub in Ireland, listening to and playing music. When they came out, they found the side window of the car had been broken—but nothing had been taken from a car full of luggage. He's convinced that a couple of Irishmen are now in rehab therapy and sworn off the drink after 'seeing' a car full of dragons and a very large Samurai in full armour.

Now this probably sounds very silly. But it works! And it does so because it subverts what Starhawk calls 'talking self', the part of us that's convinced magic is impossible. Dragons, very large bears and friendly wolves appeal to child-self, for whom nothing is impossible. Magic lives in the belief in an infinitude of possibilities.

Magic lives in the belief in an infinitude of possibilities.

If you decide to create an astral guardian in animal form, do so in as much detail as you can manage. Morwenna's dragon has a lime-green underbelly and emerald claws. Yours may be iridescent blue and silver, bright red or shining gold—it's your choice. Though I must say, I think I'd draw the line at polka-dots!

Once established, the guardian needs to be named—or, more precisely, you must ask it for its name. Remember it, but keep it secret—it is your point of contact, your PIN number if you like, and nobody else (not even your nearest and dearest) should be able to use it.

If it refuses to give you a name, tell it that you must have its name or you will return it back to the astral stuff out of which you have created it. If it continues to refuse—rare, but it can and does happen—you *must* visualise it disappearing in a puff of smoke or a burst of light. You can try again later.

Once successfully established, your guardian needs acknowledgement, and some form of payment for a job well done. Bear guardians are very fond of astral Mars Bars—and it gives you a great excuse for a little temporal treat for yourself!

Protective amulets and talismans

Protective amulets are numerous and readily available. Your choice will generally be influenced by your spiritual affiliations. Some of the most common are given below.

- **Christians** a cross or crucifix; medal of the Blessed Virgin or a saint (e.g Christopher, Benedict)
- **Muslims** a Hand of Fatima; the blue bead with a dark dot in the centre which protects against the Evil Eye
- **Jews** the Star of David (also known as the Seal of Solomon)
- **Qabalists** the glyph of the Otz Chaim, the Tree of Life
- **Hindus** the AUM symbol, the symbol of the godform of choice—Krishna, Ganesh, Kali
- **Witches, Wiccans** the Pentagram, the Celtic cross, the Cross of the Elements, the Spiral, carved stag-horn, the crescent or full Moon
- **Asatru (Norse)** the Hammer of Thor, the runes Elhaz (Eolh) and Sowelu
- **Assorted Occultists** the Rose-Cross, the Tetragrammaton, the Seal of Solomon, the Tree of Life, the Eye of Horus, the Ankh, the Buckle of Isis, the Djed of Osiris, the Feather of Ma'at

As you can see, the choice is extremely varied—and I'm sure there are other tokens I'm not familiar with or have forgotten.

All of the above are fairly easy to find. They give you the

reassurance that you are under the protection of the archetypal energy whose symbol you wear, and they advertise that protection to the people you meet. They also serve as a profession of faith, so they can be useful as a means of making contact with persons of like mind.

Precious and semi-precious stones have always been considered to be very powerful amulets for a variety of purposes—to bring luck, attract love, ensure good health.

Stones with specifically protective energies are the red ones—bloodstone, red jasper, ruby and garnet. It will come as no surprise to learn that astrologically they are those associated with Mars, the God (and planet) of War. A ruby set in iron (the metal of Mars) and made or consecrated on a Tuesday would make a very powerful Martian amulet.

Coral (often in the form of a teething ring) used to be a common gift to a new baby. Its association with Aphrodite probably expressed a wish that the child would have charm and beauty. It was also supposed to protect the child from being stolen by fairies!

The gift of a **birthstone** is the gift of an amulet of luck and protection for an infant or young adult—they are most commonly given as a christening present or as an eighteenth or twenty-first birthday gift. Most jewellers will have a list of which gems are associated with which birth date—although they should more correctly be in accordance with the person's astrological sign.

The problem here, of course, is that the realisation that a protective amulet or talisman would be really useful usually coincides with the realisation that you're in deep trouble. By the time you've found or made, and then charged, the talisman, it's either too late or the crisis is over. There are much faster ways to ask for urgent help.

The other problem—and this is true of any physical object, whether charm, amulet or talisman—is that you may easily come to believe that the magic is in the object, not in yourself.

If the object is mislaid or lost, you may believe that your protection is also lost. And of course the more energy you have put into the making and charging of a material object, the more likely you are to believe that the power is in it rather than in you. It is better to view them as an aid, a crutch that you will no longer need once you have come into your own power.

Go-away powder

My dear and good friend and teacher Paddy Slade, whose family holds a tradition of earth-magic and village witchcraft going back to before the Norman Conquest, has a secret family recipe for Go-Away Powder. Her ancestors were throwing it at the Spanish Armada, her mother and grandmother were using it against Hitler's proposed invasion of Britain after Dunkirk. This isn't the family recipe, but I have made and used my own formula effectively.

SPELL AND CHARM TO DISCOURAGE INTRUDERS

✦ Take:

- salt
- pepper
- mustard (seed or powder)
- dried hot chilis or cayenne pepper
- hyssop
- lavender
- sandalwood (powder)
- myrrh (powder)
- holly leaves (dried)
- old nettles
- thistles

✦ Pound all together in a mortar, or use a couple of plastic bags (one inside the other) and a rolling pin. The plant material is easier to grind to a powder if dried. Don't forget that you can use a microwave for quick drying—you will probably need to do so for the holly and the nettles, as your friendly local herbal supplier is unlikely to have them in stock.

You could use an electric coffee grinder, but it won't be as easy to put your energy into the compound's protective and repellent powers as it will if you pound it by hand. Elbow grease is best for this job! When the mix is finely ground enough to be scatterable, add a quantity of glitter dust (blue is good) and put it all in a jar.

✦ Charge (enspell) the mix by holding the jar in your hands and saying:

Creature of Art, I charge thee with power to keep from my door all persons or creatures who may wish me ill. Go, go, go away!

✦ Sprinkle the powder along your fence-line, across your door-sills (front and back), even along window-ledges (outside rather than in, especially if you have pets or children). Use a spoon or wear rubber gloves—it is highly irritant. Which is, of course, the object of the exercise.

✦ If you don't use all the powder, be sure to label the jar 'Go-Away Powder' or use, as I do, a skull and crossbones. You do *not* want someone adding a pinch of this to a stew!

✦ Alternatively, you could make a *charm bag* out of red felt. Fill it with the Go-Away mix and pin it over your door or hide it under a flower pot outside the door. But don't forget to specify, when charging it, that it is to keep away 'all who may wish me ill'—or you may find that not even your friends drop by for a visit any more!

Why those particular ingredients? Salt, as you should know by now, is a psychic cleanser and purifier, as are hyssop, lavender and sandalwood. Pepper, mustard and chili provide protective and deterrent energy. Myrrh is under Saturn, the planet of constraint and restriction—it is used in binding charms and incenses. Holly, nettles and thistles are all prickly, and holly was formerly used in defensive hedging—to keep stock in and marauders out. Why *old* nettles? Because they're the kind that sting. Young nettles are actually edible and can be used in soups and salads. Why the glitter dust? Mirror magic!

This is one recipe for which I don't suggest or recommend substitutions. Go out and look for the holly, the nettles and thistles—it will help focus your will.

The Correspondences

Some protective herbs are:

- **Under Mars:** Basil, chili pepper, cumin, curry leaf, damiana, dragon's blood, galangal, garlic, ginger, holly, mustard, nettle, onion, pepper, pine, thistle, tobacco.

- **Under the Sun:** Bay, benzoin, frankincense, laurel, rosemary, rowan, St Johns wort, sandalwood, sunflower.

Some purificatory herbs are:

- bay, benzoin, cedar, camomile, camphor, fennel, hyssop, lavender, lemon, rosemary, sandalwood, salt, thyme, vervain.

Protective gemstones and metals:

- **Under Mars:** gemstones: bloodstone, garnet, haematite, onyx, ruby;
  metal: iron

- **Under the Sun:** gemstones: amber, citrine, rutilated quartz (gold inclusions), tiger-eye, topaz;
  metal: gold, brass

- **For the protection of the Goddess:** gemstones: Amber, coral, jade, lapis lazuli, Venus Hair quartz, turquoise;
  metal: silver

- **Charm or mojo bags** may be red (for Mars), gold or bright yellow (for the Sun), or bright blue—electric or gas-flame blue—for the Goddess. If you can sew, you could make a bag using all these colours. Add green (also a Goddess colour) and you have a bag or pouch in the Quarter colours. What better protection could you ask for?

All plants, whether herb or spice, come from Her, no matter what their planetary correspondences, so any of the above may be used.

There are times when you just know that you are out of your depth. Other times, you may not be so sure, but life is getting, well, a bit too interesting for your liking. Playing around with a *ouija* (pronounced weeja) board, attending an uncontrolled séance, going to a ritual run by people you don't know and may be too ready to trust, can all lead to what might be called unwanted attention.

Don't be too proud to admit you've got in over your head. The rule is that Them Upstairs may not intervene in human affairs unless we ask them to do so. So *ask for help*. The most powerful invocation of assistance is the simple and fervent cry for help. You are calling in what's sometimes called the Cosmic Cavalry. Your call will not go unanswered.

Asking for help

FOR IMMEDIATE AND URGENT HELP

If it's at night, as is often the case, turn on the lights, light a candle, and ask for the protection of the Most High in whatever name or form you acknowledge him/her/it. Burn sandalwood incense. DO NOT MEDITATE—it will open the psychic centres even further—though controlling your breathing may be useful in an anxiety attack. Put on music to change the atmosphere—loud military music (massed bands, but not a single Highland piper) is really good for this. Make yourself a hot drink and a snack—this will help close down the psychic centres. If you have to sit up until dawn breaks, do so. Generally the first light will dispel the nasties and you'll be able to go back to sleep. For some reason, four in the morning is a really common time to wake in fright.

Michael (Big Mike to his friends and the less reverent amongst us) is the archangel whose particular task it is to see off the ungodly, the photophobic ones, and to protect the defenceless. His name means 'who is as God' or 'the Power of God'. 'Michael Archangel, help me!' will get an immediate response.

If you want to visualise Michael, he's usually portrayed wearing Roman military garb (helmet, red or gold breastplate, pale blue tunic, red cloak, sandals), spear in one hand and sword in the other. It's worth keeping an eye out for a good pictorial representation of the Archangel—unfortunately most of the ones I've seen (for instance, in church supply shops) show a figure of such wussitude that he wouldn't scare off a fluffy bunny. Greek or Russian Orthodox icons may be a better bet.

Incidentally, that dragon Michael is supposedly slaying wasn't originally a representation of Satan, but of earthpower and earth energy. And Michael isn't slaying it—he is controlling and directing earth energy so that it can be used productively rather than destructively (the difference, in the fire element, between a forge and a volcano, for instance).

For those of you who have problems with the Judeo-Christian associations of archangels: remember that like so many other aspects of practical magic, they have been taken over by the churches, who recognise a good thing when they see it. The angelic powers were originally a part of pre-Christian Chaldean magic. They are archetypal powers (in the Jungian sense) and you do not have to be a Christian to work with them or ask their help.

Consulting an expert

When is it time to call in a human expert? If you are experiencing:

- the sensation that you're being watched—that someone or something is lurking just outside your field of vision (but see my remarks on paranoia and anxiety attacks, above). I had just such a sensation while writing this section (at four in the morning). Fortunately my expert was in the bedroom across the hall!

- physical manifestations of nastiness:
  - foul smells (but have you checked for something dead under the floorboards and given the dog a chlorophyll tablet?)
  - poltergeist activity—objects hurtling through the air with nobody visible to do the hurling, pictures falling off walls (but check for nearness to an underground railway line, mining or blasting, earthquakes, possible subsidence of foundations)
  - noises—mad laughter, moans, shrieks—but check to make sure you haven't left the radio on in another room and that your neighbour hasn't just turned up the television

- a sudden and noticeable drop in temperature (but has there been a cool change?)
- lights flicking on and off (Check with the electricity people to see if there's an interruption of service. Make sure it's not a faulty connection. You may need an electrician, not an exorcist.)

For all of the above, in short, look for a rational explanation before you start scaring yourself silly. Once you've checked and ruled out a logical explanation, make a note (and keep a record) of what is happening, and when—i.e. day or night, at the same time of day, under what circumstances (were you asleep, in meditation, watching TV, talking to a friend about matters magical?). Whoever you consult will (or should) want to know these things.

Other manifestations that may require consultation:

- anything unseen (the seen you can usually cope with) that fills you with fear, continues to do so without apparent reason, and doesn't respond to the 'have a good laugh' technique

- if you feel overwhelmed, at the end of your tether, begin to think you're going mad, and just can't cope without help.

Remember that the events above can indicate psychological problems (paranoia, free-floating anxiety) which will respond to counselling and, in the extreme, to medication. Certainly, if you hear voices or feel inner impulses that prompt you to harm yourself or others, consult a mental health practitioner, fast. If, however, you have no previous history of such conditions, and if the symptoms seem to have come on quite suddenly, it is reasonable to wonder whether there may be more going on here than a mental or nervous breakdown.

'Who You Gonna Call?'

Don't bother looking in the phone book under 'Ghostbusters'. This is an area where personal referral is invaluable—indeed, it may be essential.

There are exorcists properly trained and authorised by their Church—most Anglican and Catholic dioceses will have at least one. The diocese may however be reluctant to admit this, or to give you a name, if you are not a churchgoer—and indeed, why should they?

If you simply decide to talk to a priest or pastor, you may find that the reception you get will depend on the nature of the parish. A church that uses incense, has a weekly sung Eucharist or High Mass, has a chapel with the Reserved Sacrament, offers holy water at the door and a place to burn votive candles, is more likely in my experience to be understanding of, shall we say, alternative spiritual experience. I know of at least one church in Melbourne that numbers shamans, high-ranking Freemasons and witches amongst its congregation.

If, on the other hand, the church is bare of ornament and ceremony, it's more likely that the incumbent will offer to pray with you to ask for help in putting the sin of occult interests behind you. This is not likely to be useful in the long term—not if the call to magic is strong. And some men claiming to be exorcists are actually dangerous. Women have been beaten to death to 'drive out the Devil' when their actual problem was untreated schizophrenia, or simply being disobedient to their husband's, their family's, or their pastor's will. So be careful who you choose to ask for help. The 'cure' may be far worse than the disease.

If you find real comfort and spiritual nourishment within your Church, don't reject it. There is a magical and mystical tradition of great richness within Christianity, if you look for it. As I have already said, prayers are spells are prayers. If returning to the Christian tradition stops the night terrors, then return, with your horizons widened. You may not be ready yet for the testing that comes with serious magic. And there's always the next life.

Any competent exorcist, whether church-based or not, will want to know the 'when/where/why' of the incidents that have brought you to ask for help—which is why it's helpful to keep a record. He will try to establish your mental state—it would be irresponsible to do otherwise. He will also want to determine whether it is a haunting of person or of place.

Hauntings of place are probably easier to deal with, because the manifestations are slightly less likely to be subjective, or open to suggestions of psychopathology. He will probably use candles, salt, holy water, incense, and prayer to cleanse the place and (if that is the cause of the problems) to send the unquiet spirit on its way.

Hauntings of person (sometimes called possession) are harder to diagnose and deal with—and much, much rarer than movies and horror novels might lead you to believe. The possibility of psychopathology (mental or emotional illness) in the victim must also be taken into consideration. It is very easy to do more harm than good.

You may have observed that I refer to 'he' and 'him'. Most exorcists are men. If you find a woman doing this kind of work, she will generally be beyond childbearing age. This does not exclude younger women from release work—the sending of a lost soul on its way home. Women are more likely to have the empathic sensitivity so useful in this kind of work.

You may realise that the disturbances that have troubled you are caused by someone who doesn't know they're dead. (This can happen if death has come unexpectedly, say, as a result of accident.) They haven't come to persecute you—it's just that you're aware of their presence, and nobody else seems to be.

Light a candle and say:

RELEASE SPELL

Go, beautiful soul, unto the place prepared for you.
In the name of the Creator who made you,
In the name of the Saviour who loves and redeems you,
In the name of the Spirit that strengthens and sanctifies you,
Go forth, go forth, go forth
To peace, and rest, and light, and joy,
Safe in the arms of the All-Loving.

Visualise a figure passing through a gateway filled with light, and being welcomed on the other side. As it passes into the light, you will feel a sense of wonder and relief. You have helped an earthbound soul to move on.

But release work is not exorcism.

Exorcism requires a degree of toughness—indeed, ruthlessness. It isn't a gentle opening of the Gates of Light and an encouragement to pass beyond. It is an absolute rejection of the will to evil, and a thrusting of that evil back to its place of origin. It requires great physical, spiritual and psychic strength.

The finest exorcists (and they are rare indeed) deal with evil by surrounding it with love and light and absorbing it into themselves—by loving it to death. It takes a lifetime (probably several) of spiritual discipline to achieve this kind of mastery. Don't try it!

So how do you know if you've found someone who's up to the job?

- Ask about his background and training—if he's not straightforward about it, doubt him. He doesn't have to be Church-trained, but Jesuits make some of the best exorcists around.

- You're entitled to ask him what he intends to do. If there's anything you're not comfortable with, say so, and ask for an explanation. Trust your instincts on the answer.

- There should be some degree of intellectual rigour in his approach. Observe what questions he asks you. It is part of his responsibility to decide whether this is a case for his skills, or those of a psychotherapist. He may well have training in both. Either way, his questioning is likely to be thorough. If, on the other hand, he seems to accept what you say without question, and encourages you to expand on the awfulness of your experience, thank him for his time and get out of there. Talking should make you feel better, not worse.

- What does he ask in payment for his services? If he wants large sums of money, or there's any suggestion that the greater your 'contribution' the more effective and long-lasting his work will be, he's a charlatan. It is of course reasonable for you to pay out-of-pocket expenses—travel costs, for instance. But the true exorcist's fee for service is likely to be to ask you to perform three acts of kindness that you wouldn't normally do. The first should be to pray for the person (dead or alive) who's given you the grief. As long as you continue in resentment you provide a path for them back to you and your life.

The last word

One of the difficulties about writing on psychic protection and self-defence is that describing a state or set of symptoms may actually encourage the anxieties you hope to dispel. There are at least two books on the subject that had me looking over my shoulder and checking the corners of the room within minutes of opening them. I hope that this section has not had that effect on its readers.

Chapter Seven

kitchen witchery: the magic of food

Good food is one of life's great pleasures. It's also yet another way of putting some magic into your life.

Like colours, gemstones, herbs and perfumes, certain foods fall under certain planetary influences. Most spices, for example, are governed by either Mars (hot and fiery spices—mustard, chili, garlic) or Jupiter (allspice, cinnamon, nutmeg). Herbs tend to be governed by Mercury or Venus. Most white food, and/or food with a high water content (milk, cucumber, potato) is governed by the Moon. Most fruits—especially sweet fruits—are under the influence of Venus. Vegetables are governed by different planets, but because they come out of the earth will all partake of that element. Especially if eaten with the abundance of Gaia in mind, they will all encourage abundance-consciousness.

What makes food magical? Magical intent!

It is both possible and practical to devise individual dishes, or indeed a whole meal, directed towards a magical intent—abundance, money, love, protection. As well as choosing your ingredients with their planetary correspondence in mind, you need also to focus on your intention during the food's preparation.

The simplest way to do this is to light a candle of the appropriate colour (see Chapter Three) and state your intention before starting to prepare the food. It's a little like saying Grace—but before preparation rather than before eating. You can be quite specific and say *The food that I prepare draws* (state your purpose—abundance, protection) *to me and mine*, or use something more general such as:

ABUNDANCE SPELL

Gaia, Lady and Mother, Giver of all good things
Give with this food health and wealth and knowledge
Nurturing us with your abundant and protective love
As I prepare it with love.
So be it. So be it. So be it.

You can of course make your prayer or say your spell to 'Lord and Father' if you wish.

Food so prepared is what a Hindu would call *prasad*. They consider all prepared food is consecrated to the gods; we partake of their leftovers. Or, you might say, we share in their feasting. One thing I have observed is that food prepared in this way, in a state of mindfulness and as an act of conscious reverence, tastes different—better, more alive.

From mysticism to practicality. What do we cook in order to achieve a particular end—to draw money, love, protection and other good and necessary things into home and family life?

Food for abundance and money

In Chapter Five, there's a Jupiter Money-Drawing Mix which includes cinnamon, cloves, mustard seed, and nutmeg, together with other plant substances under the influence of Jupiter. Those spices, with the addition of pepper, ginger, sweet paprika, chili, cumin, coriander (all under Mars) and fenugreek seeds and turmeric (under Mercury, ruler of commerce and communications) will make a very good curry mix and draw abundance, vitality and protection at the same time. Now that's kitchen witchery!

MONEY-DRAWING CURRY MIX

✧ Make sure all the spices are as fresh as possible. Supermarket spices can be stale, so it's worth tracking down an Indian grocery or Middle Eastern nut shop to ensure freshness. Proportions are very much to taste, but I'd suggest a tablespoon each of cinnamon, mustard seed, sweet paprika, cumin, and coriander; a dessertspoon each of pepper and fenugreek seeds; and a teaspoon each of cloves (powdered cloves will do), dried chili, nutmeg and turmeric. Mix all together, visualising money pouring into the mixing bowl, while be-spelling the spices with:

Spices of Jupiter and of Mars
Mercury too, find what I seek!
Cinnamon, pepper and fenugreek

Cumin and chili, coriander, clove,
Gathered from fragrant tree and grove,
Nutmeg sweet and mustard sharp
Turmeric, colour of bright gold
Mix and mingle, bring me wealth!
Bring me favour, bring me flavour,
Bring me good things through my door!

✦ Transfer contents to a storage jar and use when making a curry. Ginger is a great addition. You can add powdered ginger (2 tbsp) to the mix, but I prefer to use the fresh root.

TO MAKE A MONEY-DRAWING CURRY

Choose what you're going to curry. Eggplant is ruled by Jupiter and draws money to you—in fact, there's a little money-drawing charm that involves slicing an eggplant down its length, putting in a dollar, tying the two halves back together, and burying the bundle under an oak tree (also sacred to Jupiter). An eggplant bhaji (dry curry) has the advantage of not wasting the eggplant—or the dollar.

Pumpkin is ruled by the Sun, the other great abundance-bringer. The pumpkin's roundness and golden colour emphasise its money-drawing power. Spinach is also under Jupiter, so a combination of pumpkin and spinach, perhaps with the addition of raw cashew nuts (also under the rulership of the Sun and a money-attractor) would make another dish both tasty and magical.

Sauté several onions (Mars, protection, vitality) in ghee or oil until soft and beginning to caramelise. Add chopped fresh ginger and chopped or crushed fresh garlic (both under Mars). Don't use ginger or garlic pastes-in-a-jar unless desperate—they don't have the energy of the fresh product. Sauté briefly. Then add two tablespoons (or thereabouts—adjust to taste) of the Money-Drawing Curry Mix. Fry to energise the spices and release their oils—they should begin to smell fragrant. Add a tin of chopped tomatoes to bring charm to the dish (they're under Venus) and allow to simmer until the flavours have had a chance to mingle.

For eggplant bhaji: cube the eggplant, sprinkle with salt to extract any bitter juices. Put in a colander and leave to drain for half an hour, then squeeze out—or use the small Lebanese eggplants, which won't need salting. Fry until golden. Add as much of the curry sauce (above) as you think right—it shouldn't be swimming in sauce; a bhaji is a dry curry. Stir through and serve.

For the pumpkin, spinach and cashew nut curry: add the cubed pumpkin and raw cashews to the curry sauce, and simmer until the pumpkin is cooked and the cashews are plump. Stir in the spinach at the last minute, so it keeps its lovely green colour. Serve up as soon as the spinach is wilted.

You may care to serve these with Celebration Rice.

CELEBRATION RICE

This is a money-drawing rice pilau with raisins, cashews, slivered almonds, pine nuts, sesame seeds and sunflower seeds (buy the nuts at the same time as you buy the fresh spices). Everything in it is under the planetary influence of the Sun or of Jupiter. It goes well with curries, or—topped with sliced hard-boiled eggs, symbol of fertility, eternity and perfection—as a meal on its own.

✦ Pre-cook the rice and allow to stand and drain awhile—it shouldn't be too wet. Melt ghee or a mix of olive oil and butter in a wok, and add the nuts and seeds. Stir until toasted and starting to colour—watch like a hawk, as they go from toasted to burnt in a couple of seconds. Add the raisins or sultanas, which will start to swell in the heat. Then add the pre-cooked rice and stir through. Add salt or seasoned salt to taste. (Vegeta is very good in this dish.) If serving to accompany a curry, serve as is. If serving as a main dish, you may care to add a spoonful of cinnamon or Money-Drawing Curry Mix to the dish. You can also colour the rice with true saffron for added oomph.

Other abundance and money-drawing foods

GREEN VEGETABLES

Green vegetables are all money attractants. Cabbage, and indeed the whole *brassica* family—brussel sprouts, broccoli, cauliflower—will draw money to you. They will also, with the addition of some culinary imagination, feed you well and inexpensively—another way of accessing abundance. Try an old Irish favourite, colcannon, for a satisfying and money-drawing dish with a Celtic flavour.

COLCANNON

✧ Fry some rashers of bacon—streaky is best for this dish—in a little butter. Add cubed, pre-cooked potatoes, sauté until golden. Add finely shredded raw cabbage, toss through. Add salt and pepper to taste. Eat piping hot, while the cabbage still has some crunch to it.

✧ In Ireland they pile the colcannon in a mound, make a dint in the top, and put a chunk of butter in it to melt through the dish. Cholesterol hell, tastebud heaven.

Spinach, as we've already seen, is under the rulership of Jupiter. If you associate spinach with slimy green pondweed, adjust your tastebuds. Try a dish called *horenso* next time you're in a Japanese restaurant. It's a roll of spinach and sesame seed so fresh and verdant that it squeaks when you bite it.

When cooking spinach at home, the secret is in not overcooking it—if you do it will indeed become slimy and horrid. Don't use water, except to wash the spinach before wilting it in a little butter or oil. Flavour with nutmeg or sprinkle with sesame seed to attract money. Or don't cook it at all. Fry some bacon, deglaze the pan with a good vinegar (wine or balsamic) and pour the whole as a dressing over baby spinach leaves to make a first-rate, abundance-drawing salad.

At the other end of the scale, all rich and expensive foods are at least in part under the rulership of Jupiter. Salmon is food of the sea, and therefore ruled by Venus; but the luxuriousness of smoked salmon brings it firmly into the realm of Jupiter. Milk may be under the rulership of the Moon, but cream in all its lusciousness is Jupiterian.

CHOCOLATE

Chocolate is Jupiterian, although the individual ingredients—sugar, cocoa, cocoa butter, and vanilla—are under the rulership of Mars (cocoa) and Venus (sugar, vanilla). This puts Mars and Venus, those two archetypal lovers, in very close conjunction indeed, and may partly account for chocolate's reputation as an aphrodisiac.

The reputation might be well deserved. Recent research indicates that some of the chemical elements present in chocolate are also present in the body after a satisfying orgasm! It would seem that chocolate in all its various forms—eating and drinking chocolate, chocolate mud cake, chocolate syrup, chocolate milk—is very much the food of love. Maybe the combination of Jupiter, Mars and Venus makes chocolate the secret of abundant love. You can never have too much of a good thing!

NUTS

Most nuts are under the rulership of Jupiter or the Sun—cashews, hazelnuts, peanuts, walnuts and macadamias—as are raisins. So if you have a weakness for chocolate-coated peanuts or raisins, you can indulge your passion while muttering

Jupiter, Mars and Venus
Bring me luck, bring me wealth, bring me love!

If, on the other hand, you're studying hard and want a feel-good fix while adding to your brain power, munch on some chocolate-coated almonds. Almonds are ruled by Mercury, and are considered to be a brain food (as indeed are walnuts, because of their resemblance to that organ). Since Mercury governs commerce as well as communication, the almond is also believed to be money-drawing. The other nut associated with wisdom is of course the hazelnut, which in Celtic tradition was the sole food of the Salmon of Wisdom.

The peanuts don't have to be chocolate-coated, of course—a peanut-butter sandwich on oat bread, perhaps with the addition of cumquat marmalade (cumquats are traditionally money-drawing because they're round and golden), will bring abundance to your lunch box. Or you can go for that playground favourite, peanut butter and sultana sandwiches, on multi-grain bread to combine Jupiter and the Sun with the sustaining energy of Earth.

GRAINS AND SEEDS

Grains and seeds would seem to fall naturally under the auspices of Demeter, the Greek Earth-Mother—and the elemental ruler of Earth. In terms of their planetary rulership, they tend to be associated with the expansiveness of either Jupiter or the Sun (except for rye and wheat, which are ruled by Venus). In Celtic wisecraft, of course, they are all the gift of the Cauldron of Ceridwen. Whatever their ruler, grains and seeds spell abundance.

Sesame seeds are the ultimate good-fortune seed. They are under the rulership of the Sun and the Element of Fire. They're very prolific as well. Sprinkle on foods (such as spinach) to draw money, luck, protection and good sex. Choose a sesame bagel for your lunch. Fill it with sweet peppers and hot salami for protection, or avocado and chicken to honour Venus and draw love to you. A topping of baba ghanoush (eggplant and tahina—ground sesame seeds) will give you a triple whammy in the money-drawing and abundance stakes. I also add sesame seeds to all charms 'to open doors'.

Any bread, biscuits, pancakes or breakfast cereals made of barley, buckwheat, corn, oats, millet, rice or rye will help draw abundance into your life—as long as you eat them in full consciousness of that intent. Chocolate puffed rice is one way to go, though in terms of nutritional value a bowl of porridge will not only get your day off to a flying start, abundance-wise, but act as a calmative on a busy day. That Aussie favourite, the Anzac biscuit, with its combination of oats, butter and golden syrup, makes a great abundance-drawing midmorning snack.

Scott Cunningham, in *The Magic in Food*, suggests making up a buckwheat pancake batter (you can find a premix in your supermarket), pouring it on to your griddle or hotplate in the shape of a dollar sign, and eating it with maple syrup (also under the rulership of Jupiter).

I would favour an old-fashioned Aussie **rice pudding**. To a cup of round grain rice, add two cups of milk (or a little more).

Stir in sugar or honey, cinnamon, nutmeg and raisins (all under Jupiter). Dot with a little butter. Cook in a slow oven for about 40 minutes. This will help abundance in a very practical way—it's comfort food, nurturing, and much less expensive than supermarket desserts! But if you want something a little special and more extravagant, use chopped glacé fruit (apricots, oranges, peaches) instead of (or as well as) the raisins, and serve with cream. Or you could try:

MONEY TRIFLE

Scott Cunningham recommends this one.

- 1 cup of either chopped peach, mango, banana, pineapple, thinly sliced pear, or blackberries—or a mix of these
- 4 cups sponge cake (stale is fine) cut into cubes
- sherry or kirsch to taste—or use orange juice, or both.
- 1 cup prepared custard
- 1 cup whipped cream.

✦ Put half the sponge cake in a bowl, moisten well with half the sherry (or orange juice, or both). Add fruit. Add rest of sponge cake, sprinkle with rest of sherry and/or juice. Pour custard over the whole. Top with whipped cream and additional fruit, leave to refrigerate overnight or for at least six hours.

I'd add toasted slivered almonds and shaved chocolate (dark, of course) to the top just before serving—and probably put more sherry in the trifle itself. Or you could try a recipe that all my friends expect me to make come Summer Solstice. All dried fruit is under the rulership of the Sun (unsurprisingly), as is red wine such as port—so this is a real abundance-consciousness-raising dessert.

QUEENSLAND COLD CHRISTMAS PUDDING: SUMMER SOLSTICE DELIGHT

✦ Take an assortment of dried fruits—mixed fruit, raisins, figs, apricots, apple, prunes, cherries—chop the larger ones (or use a pre-chopped fruit medley mix), and cover them all with whatever alcohol you have to hand. A mix of sherry, port and brandy is good. Leave for 24 hours so that the fruit has absorbed all or most of the liquid.

✦ Dissolve two packets of port wine jelly in the amount of water specified for one packet (i.e. so you have double-strength jelly). Allow it to cool slightly (you cool the jelly so the alcohol doesn't evaporate) and add to the fruit. Put in the fridge for 24 hours to allow time to set. (If you've used too much hooch, as I did one year, it may refuse to set and you may have to add gelatine, or put it in the freezer for a while before serving.)

✦ Serve in **small** portions (it is extremely rich and pretty alcoholic) with the best cream or ice-cream you can find. Watch your guests slither quietly under the table with happy smiles on their faces.

✦ It is of course both ethical and prudent to warn guests beforehand of the pud's alcohol content—some medications don't mix with alcohol, and a good serve may also tip a driver over the legal limit.

At Winter Solstice, on the other hand, you should serve **mulled wine** to warm the body and reassure the soul that the Sun will return after the shortest day of the year. It is also, given the combination of spices, red wine and orange slices, a great encourager of abundance-consciousness and should draw money into your vicinity as well as friends into your home.

MULLED WINE

Take spices of Jupiter, and of Mars too—
Nutmeg, cinnamon, allspice and clove
Add honey or sugar to sweeten the brew,
And sweet orange slices, fruit of the grove.
Put in a saucepan and add red wine—
A wine good enough, but not the best,
And simmer awhile with fruit and the rest
Until all is mingled and tastes divine.
Then take off the fire, pour in more wine
And serve it forth to warm the hearts
And hands, and feet, and other parts
That Winter's chill has made to pine.
And drink the Sun's health in good mulled wine!

Not a mention so far of meat, I hear the carnivores amongst you cry. No, this is not a vegetarian plot. Nor do you have to be a vegetarian to follow a spiritual or magical path. Eat what suits your digestion. But in case you're wondering what goes with what, Patricia Telesco, in her excellent and practical *A Kitchen Witch's Cookbook*, assigns the following significances to produce of the animal kingdom:

- beef—prosperity, grounding
- cheese—joy, health, things coming to fruition
- chicken—health, wellbeing, sunrise magic
- fish—love, sex life
- ham—theatrical flair, dramatic energy
- lamb—sensitivity, kindness, warmth
- pork—fertility, profuseness
- sausage—zest, variety, good magic
- turkey—colourful displays, holiday feasts.

I'd add to this that turkey, in the Native American tradition, is strongly connected to the idea of sharing abundance. The custom of *potlatch*, from which the word 'potluck' is derived, involves a feast at which possessions are given away to other, needier members of the tribe or social group. It's been taken into general American custom in the form of the 'potluck supper', to which every guest contributes a dish and all food is shared.

In Australia we call it 'bringing a plate' or, in New Age and Pagan circles, bringing food to share. Whatever you call it, it encourages abundance-consciousness in demonstrating that there is enough, and more than enough, food and good fellowship to go around.

Meat generally is both energising and grounding. This is probably the main practical reason for its exclusion from the diets of religious orders of various faiths. It is easier to follow a life of constant prayer and meditation if your connection to your body is somewhat attenuated. A vegetarian diet can of course be both well-balanced and grounding, especially if it is rich in grains, pulses and root vegetables. As I said earlier, eat what suits your digestion and your temperament.

A major exclusion from Patricia Telesco's list is game of all sorts—rabbit, game fowl such as pheasant, partridge and grouse, and of course venison. The stag occupies a position of particular importance in the myth and folklore of the Celtic tradition. He is the animal symbol or totem of the God—Cernunnos, Herne the Hunter—who sacrifices himself so that the people may live.

Game is generally hunted in the colder half of the year, and in early times was often the major, and sometimes the only, source of meat protein for the clan. The stag and the boar or wild pig were both culturally and spiritually significant to the Celtic and pre-Celtic peoples of the British Isles, and are both associated with the Midwinter festivals.

One of the best-known pieces of Medieval music is the 'Boar's Head Carol', sung when the boar's head (accompanied by the rest of the pig) was brought in solemn procession into the feasting hall. Another carol, 'The Holly and the Ivy', has as part of its refrain: 'the rising of the sun and the running of the deer', and has strong links to Arthur, the Once and Future King of the Isles of the Mighty.

I am a stag of seven tines ...
I am a boar, ruthless and red ...
I am a wizard: who but I
Sets the cool head aflame with smoke?

from *Song of Amergin*

The stag of seven tines was considered the food of kings and emperors. We don't have to be of the blood royal to eat venison now, although we may have to hunt for it—from a specialist butcher, usually! It's worth tracking some down for a special Winter Solstice celebration. Serve with mulled wine to welcome back the Sun.

WINTER SOLSTICE VENISON CASSEROLE

✧ You need to allow about three days to prepare this dish. Take stewing venison enough for the company, and marinate for twenty-four hours in Guinness or your preferred stout, together with a dozen or so juniper berries and some peppercorns, which have been crushed to release the oils and the flavour, and crushed garlic to taste.

✧ After marinating, drain the meat, saving the marinade mix. Sauté onions, carrots and celery, all finely chopped, in a little butter and oil. Toss the venison in flour, add it to the vegetables, and let it brown. Pour in the reserved marinade and cook, very slowly, for several hours until the meat is tender—overnight in a slow cooker does very well. You may want to thicken the gravy with a little more flour before serving.

✧ I like to add Chinese dried mushrooms—pre-soaked and sliced—to this dish. If you prefer, add whole button mushrooms or, better still, field mushrooms, about halfway through the cooking time. (Mushrooms, incidentally, are supposed to heighten psychic awareness. They're under the rulership of the Moon.)

Serve with **sesame potatoes** for a Midwinter feast fit for King Arthur's court—except that he didn't have potatoes, poor man, and would have had to be content with a purée of turnips and parsnips. Sesame seeds, as we have already seen, are ruled by the Sun and are money-drawing. Potatoes, like all root vegetables, partake of the abundance of the Element of Earth, as well as being ruled by the Moon because of their colour and high water content. The combination is therefore both magical and well-balanced, as well as delicious.

SESAME POTATOES

❖ Take more potatoes than you think you and your guests could possibly eat—this is a dish that has them saying 'Oh, isn't there any more?' Peel, or if the skins look OK, just scrub the spuds. Then slice them about a centimetre thick, keeping the shape of the spud. Put in a baking dish so that the slices are layered at an angle. Drizzle with olive oil, sprinkle lavishly with sesame seeds—they should coat the upper edges of the potatoes. Salt and pepper (or use a seasoning salt such as Vegeta) and put into a hot oven for about 45 minutes. The edges will be crisp, and the rest soft and luscious. Yum!

By now you should be feeling (or preparing to feel) both well-fed and abundance-conscious. Time to take a look at some other appetites.

'If music be the food of love ...'

Music may be the food of love, but so is, well, food! And it would seem that love demands its just desserts—especially if the dessert is fruit-based.

Most sweet and soft fruits—strawberries, raspberries, cherries, peaches, plums, apricots—are under the rulership of Venus/Aphrodite. What more luscious than a perfectly ripe peach or nectarine? What is more of an aphrodisiac than rich dark cherries, or the perfume of perfectly ripe strawberries? The perfect breakfast for abundance-conscious lovers would have to be cinnamon toast topped with fresh strawberries and cream. For an Aphrodisian dessert, try strawberries dipped in dark chocolate—see **chocolate**, above. Or a sinfully rich chocolate mousse garnished with sliced strawberries and whipped cream.

Bananas are however ruled by Mars, which given their shape, is hardly surprising. Strawberries and sliced banana, combining Mars and Venus, make a great start to the day, or an end to a perfect lovers' meal.

Apples are the fruit most often eaten to honour the Goddess. When cut across the middle, the pattern of seeds reveals Her pentagram. Paddy Slade's Apple Charm, to keep lovers faithful, instructs you to cut an apple in half across the middle and to write your names, one on each half. Put the two halves back together and bind round with red silk (embroidery) thread. Bury the apple where it will not be disturbed (I'd suggest under an apple tree). You and your love will remain true to each other. But remember the Law—as you bind, so you are bound. Don't expect an easy time of it if your body or mind gets the itch for someone new.

It's probably safer to slice some apples and sauté them in butter until they're starting to brown slightly. Sprinkle with a very little brown sugar and some dark rum, shake the pan to mix and mingle—they will form a toffee—like sauce—and serve with cream. The way to a man's heart, proverbially, is through his stomach. Or you can eat and enjoy these Buttered Rum Apples as a private luxury. Take the peel off one of the apples in a single, unbroken piece and throw it over your shoulder to form the initial of the man who will become your own true love.

The apple is sacred to Aphrodite, and so is the **quince**, used in love magic by some European Romanies. Quinces also ward off evil, and their fragrance will perfume your kitchen and draw in positive energy of all kinds. They must however be cooked to be edible. Peel, core, slice, and simmer in a sugar syrup—they turn the most beautiful ruby-red colour. I suspect the Gypsy love-magic probably involved feeding this dish to the man you wished to attract. The colour would be a clear signal to him of your passionate temperament and your interest in receiving his attentions.

Any good book of jams and jellies will have a recipe for quince jelly. Again, the beauty of its colour alone makes it worth having on your pantry shelf. For something a little different, try a Gypsy conserve known in Portugal as *marmelo.*

MARMELO

✦ Take quinces, peel, quarter and core them. Steam the quarters until they are soft. Purée them, then weigh them. Take an equal weight of sugar, and put quince purée and sugar into a preserving pan or heavy-based saucepan. Cook over a gentle heat until the mixture starts to pull away from the sides of the pan. It will have darkened slightly, but be careful not to let it burn. Turn the mixture out on to a baking tray that you have previously lined with lightly oiled greaseproof paper, smooth out with a palette knife, and leave to cool and set. Cut into cubes and toss in a little caster sugar—the marmelo should be quite dry, the sugar just helps keep the cubes separate.

✦ Marmelo is traditionally served as an accompaniment to cheese, as we might serve grapes or slices of apple or pear.

The following Fruit Salad Love Spell is quoted by Scott Cunningham in his book *The Magic in Food*:

FRUIT SALAD LOVE SPELL

Fruit of mango, fruit of pine,
Let the one I love be mine.
Fruit of apple, fruit of peach,
Bring him (her) close within my reach.
Fruit of banana, fruit of cherry,
Let his (her) love for me not vary.
As I work my magic spell
Warmly in his (her) heart I dwell.
I now invoke the Law of Three
This is my will, so mote it be!

✦ You are instructed to make the salad while concentrating on the love you wish to share. Chant the spell as you chop and slice.

The fruits specified are under the rulership of Mars (banana, mango), the Sun (pineapple) or Venus (the rest), so astrologically the spell should work. But the combination of flavours isn't to my taste—they seem to have been chosen for rhyme rather than reason. And I'm not too sure about the ethics of this spell—there's a strong element of compulsion in the wording. Be sure your intention is to share rather than compel love—or the Law of Three may give you more than you bargained for, or wanted (see Chapter Four on the subject of ethics in love magic).

Finally, a fresh, ripe mango is such a luscious treat eaten on its own that I feel it would be wasted in a fruit salad. And we mango addicts are reluctant to share a mango even with our best-beloveds—let them get their own, we say!

The fruit salad could however also offer protection as well as love—both the Sun and Mars have protection as well as maleness within their purview. Pineapple is considered to be especially protective, its prickly leaves and outer coat guarding the sweetness within. It's also given health-inducing properties. It will certainly soothe a sore throat, and seems to have some antiseptic properties as well.

If you wanted to add further to the fruit salad's protective aspect, the addition of orange slices or juice would assist, and also add a touch of the Sun's abundance. A sprinkling of orange flower water over the salad might even encourage him to propose—the perfume of orange flowers has been associated with weddings since Tudor times, when they began to be introduced into the bridal bouquet. Orange flower water or rose water (obtainable from Middle Eastern groceries) will also add a delectable fragrance to slices of watermelon.

Enough of all this fruit! What **vegetables** might encourage an abundance of love in your life?

Sweet potato is well regarded in the encouragement-of-love department. It's a root vegetable—a good start. It's governed by Venus. The combination of Earth and Venus suggests that it will encourage love that is well founded, supportive, and gentle. Cooking sweet potatoes with a honey glaze is the way to go. This recipe is based on a Jewish dish, *tzimmes*, traditionally eaten at

New Year *(Rosh Hashonah)*, when the golden colour and sweetness are supposed to encourage a sense of prosperity. The use of apples and honey adds to its Aphrodisian potential. It would be a good dish to serve at Autumn Equinox or Lammas, the Celtic harvest festivals.

HARVEST HEAVEN SWEET POTATOES

- ½ cup honey
- ¼ cup olive oil
- ½ teaspoon grated lemon rind
- ½ teaspoon grated orange rind
- 6 cups diced sweet potato
- 3 apples, peeled and sliced
- salt and pepper to taste

✦ Preheat oven to approx 175 degrees Celsius (350 degrees Fahrenheit). Put the apples and sweet potato in a well-oiled baking dish. Mix the honey, oil and orange and lemon zests (a microwave is very useful for liquefying honey), pour over, and stir through well. Season with salt and pepper, and a little nutmeg or cinnamon if liked. Cover and bake until the sweet potatoes are tender—about 35 minutes. Bake, uncovered, for a further 5–10 minutes, until golden brown.

Tomatoes were deemed to be highly aphrodisiacal when they were first introduced to Europe from the New World. Indeed, they used to be called 'Love Apples'—a name that still finds echoes in the French *pomme d'amour*, and the Italian *pomodoro*.

They are, of course, governed by Venus. Eat them fresh—picked and juicy, still warm from the sun, perhaps with a sprinkling of sugar to emphasise their natural sweetness, and it's easy to understand their erotic potential.

Tomatoes will also draw money, health, and protection—depending on how and with what they are combined. To attract money, eat them with basil—a perfect combination. For a protective zap and zing, combine them with garlic, onion, sweet peppers, and lots of chili, thus making a *salsa arrabiata* to spice up your pasta and your love life.

And speaking of spices . . .

LOUISE HUEBNER'S SPICE BLEND

- 1 tsp cumin
- 1 tsp mace
- 1 tsp sage
- 1 tsp thyme
- a pinch of rosemary
- 1 tsp cloves
- 1 tsp nutmeg
- 1 tbsp ginger

✧ Mix or grind together. Use only fresh spices. Use as a body rub to arouse lust.

Yes, well, maybe. It'd give a new meaning to 'You smell good enough to eat'. I'd be more inclined to rub the mix on a chicken or a leg of lamb before roasting it. Serve with sesame roast potatoes, spinach with nutmeg, and a glass of mead for an all-round abundant love feast. Or you could warm powdered coriander seeds in wine to stimulate desire—it would also assist digestion, no bad thing after a heavy meal.

All seafood is under the rulership of Venus, so a spaghetti marinara or a whole fish baked with a tomato sauce would be distinctly Aphrodisian—as indeed are oysters, though I think they should be eaten *au naturel.*

So much for Venus. What about Mars? He is the lover (but not the husband) of Venus in classical mythology. He's also the God of War. So here the boundary between love and protection starts to blur somewhat.

Asparagus has long had a reputation as an aphrodisiac. Certainly its shape and general perkiness makes this an easy metaphor to grasp, as it were. Eat it lightly steamed—don't overcook, or it will go limp—with butter or a vinaigrette sauce.

Casanova swore by **celery** as a stimulant to flagging lust—see Chapter Four for Casanova's Celery Tonic. Celery is under the rulership of Mercury, he of the winged sandals—the name itself derives from the Latin *celeriter*, 'faster'. One hopes that the speed is not of the 'wham, bam, thank you, ma'am' kind. Perhaps it's possible to slow your chap down by combining the celery with potato in a sustaining soup.

Originally, of course, like many foods from the New World, **potatoes** were believed to be highly aphrodisiac—Shakespeare refers to them in this context. Flavour your potato and celery soup with garlic and onions for their protective power. This could give a new meaning to safe sex!

Chilis are also under the rulership of Mars, but their role is primarily protective. Add to dishes designed to protect you and yours against negative energies. *Chili con carne*, which combines prosperity (beans), love (tomatoes) and protection (chilis, cumin, onions and garlic), is a way to go.

CHILI CON CARNE CON ATTITUDE

✦ Chop two or three large onions and several cloves of garlic, and fry in olive oil until golden. Add a good pinch of cumin, marjoram, and a finely chopped sweet red pepper and a tablespoon of sweet paprika. Add chili peppers to your taste. If you like your food on the searing side of spicy, use birdseye or *habanero* chilis. But all the chili family have protective qualities—the sweet as well as the fiery varieties. So if you can't stand the heat, you don't have to get out of the kitchen. Just use sweet peppers instead.

✦ Add the meat—½ kg of beef, though in Mexico they also use pork and chicken—and stir through. Allow it to brown, then add red kidney beans—the red colour is protective, and beans encourage prosperity (perhaps because they are cheap and filling). You can pre-soak and pre-cook the beans, but adding a large tin of them, drained and rinsed, is fine. Add a tin of chopped tomatoes, and some tomato paste for added richness. Salt and pepper to taste, and your protective and abundant supper is ready to eat. Vegetarians can of course omit the meat (in which case it becomes chili *sans* carne), but should eat the dish with rice or tortillas for a balanced meal.

Leeks are ruled by Mars and are partly responsible for the randy reputation of the Welsh (the ones who aren't too busy singing, that is). They're also protective and are supposed to defend against lightning strikes. Welsh soldiers rubbed the juice on their bodies to add to their physical (virile) strength and protect against wounds.

Onions and **garlic** (the other alliums) are deemed to have the same protective virtue as the leek. A halved onion, kept in the kitchen, was believed to absorb evil. And, of course, the antipathy of vampires to garlic is well known.

Protective Foods

The first question to ask here is protection from whom, and for what reason. If you are or believe yourself to be in need of physical protection—you're a victim of domestic violence, for example, or you think someone is stalking you—don't waste time eating protective foods. Get the hell out of there, go to the police, go to a refuge. And take self-defence lessons.

If the threat is more intangible, for strategies see Chapter Six. But it's also possible to add to your sense of safety (itself a great protection) by adding protective herbs and spices to your food. Pepper, chili, garlic, mustard, horseradish, paprika, parsley, and rosemary all have their part to play.

If adding a number of these, you can pile them on a piece of paper and trace a banishing pentagram in them before adding them to food. However, they will perhaps be more palatable in a salad dressing than sprinkled into a pot of beans or a stew.

PROTECTIVE SALAD DRESSING

✦ Take some or all of the protective herbs and spices given above, place in a jar, and add olive oil (for the protective power of the Sun) and good vinegar (ruled by Saturn, the planet of constriction—to bind your oppressor) together with a little salt. Shake all together until emulsified while saying:

Let no harm come nigh me
All good will surround me
Spice and herb protect me
Keep me safe and free!

✦ Use as a salad dressing. It would be particularly good on a warm potato salad to which chopped hard-boiled eggs have been added. Or use it to dress:

Fiery Protection salad

- ½ head red cabbage
- 1 red capsicum
- 1 red onion
- 2 radishes

✦ Finely slice all ingredients, mix, and add Protective Salad Dressing. This would be good as an accompaniment to *chili con carne.*

If you have some idea of the direction from which the threat is coming, use the same combination of pepper, chili, garlic, mustard, horseradish, paprika, parsley, and rosemary (in their dry or powdered form) as a go-away powder. Use the mix to draw a pentagram on the window ledge, point outwards (directing the energy towards the oppressor). Then place a round mirror upright on the ledge, also facing the direction of the threat, on top of the pentagram. Say, with as much force and conviction as you can muster:

Go from my window, go from my door
Go from my life, trouble me no more!

If this spell can wait until the moon is waning, so much the better—but if the need is great, do it anyway. Obviously, don't do this unless you really mean it.

The Chinese and Japanese place sprays of peach or plum blossom at doors to ward off evil. Plants generally are good *feng shui*, and a nice prickly cactus or spiky agave or aloe on the window ledge (use the spell above) will add protective energy to your living space. Mexicans believe that fresh coriander leaves will ward off evil. So will fresh basil. And you can use it in:

PROTECTIVE PIZZA

✦ Use fresh tomatoes or get a bottle of *passata di pomodori* and add basil, black pepper and parsley—chili too, if you like it. Pour on to the base. (Pizza bases, without topping, are available from your supermarket or Italian deli; or you can make your own.) Put five pieces of chive (or spring onion) on top in the shape of a pentagram. Add sweet peppers, artichoke hearts, cheese, garlic, hot salami or whatever other protective food you like. Cook and eat.

If you make your own biscuits, you can cut them out in shape of a protective pentagram. Sprinkle savoury biscuits with paprika, cayenne or pepper before baking. Mark discs of sweet or savoury biscuits, before baking, with the Celtic equal-armed cross (the Cross of the Elements) to draw the protection of earth, air, fire, water and spirit into your life and your body. As you do so, or when you eat them, say:

Earth sustain me
Water uphold me
Fire encourage me
Air uplift me
Spirit enfold me
Five of Power, keep me safe!

You can use this spell when preparing any food, or as a protective mantra at any time.

I'm not sure where Hildegarde of Bingen's Intelligence Cookies fit into the scheme of things. Maybe it's a case of enhance your capacity for clear thinking, and all else follows.

Hildegarde of Bingen was one intelligent cookie herself. She ran one of the largest abbeys in Medieval Germany, the equivalent in our day to being the head of a multinational corporation. She also wrote books on diet, medicine, theology, and spiritual devotions. She painted, she wrote music and supervised its performance. She travelled constantly. She gave advice to popes and bishops, whether they wanted it or not.

If she hadn't been such a devout and influential Christian, she would probably have been burned as a witch. It was ever thus.

This is a modernised version of her recipe for Intelligence Cookies. It makes about three hundred biscuits.

HILDEGARDE'S INTELLIGENCE COOKIES

- 1½ cups of butter
- 3 cups of brown sugar
- 2 eggs, well-beaten
- ½ teaspoon salt
- 4 teaspoons baking powder
- 6 cups plain flour

- 2¼ teaspoons nutmeg
- ½ teaspoon ground cloves
- 2 teaspoons grated lemon zest
- 1 cup ground almond meal

✦ Cream butter and sugar until light and fluffy. Add eggs and lemon zest. Sift in remaining ingredients, mix in and knead together. Shape into rolls, wrap in waxed paper, and chill thoroughly. When firm, slice thin and bake in a quick (moderately hot) oven until lightly browned (about ten minutes). You may like to mark each disc with a Cross of the Elements before baking.

Take a cup of Earl Grey tea with your Intelligence Cookies—the fragrance of bergamot oil helps clear the mind. Both tea and coffee are under the rulership of Mars (they are stimulants) but their fragrance is definitely Mercurial. Try a single drop of pure peppermint oil (not peppermint essence) in your morning coffee as a wake-up call. But don't think that if one drop is good, two will be better. Two will be undrinkable.

RULERSHIP OF HERBS AND SPICES

- allspice—Jupiter. Luck, money, good health.
- anise—Jupiter. Encourages loving relationships.
- basil—Mars. A sacred herb to the ancient Greeks and Hindus. Attracts love, money.
- bay—Apollo, the Sun. Health, good fortune, honour.
- cardamom—Venus. Love, sex. Add to coffee. Increases the strength of partnership.

- chives—Mercury/Mars. Protection, breaking bad habits.
- cinnamon—Jupiter/Sun. Love and money. Add to coffee to draw money.
- clove—Jupiter, fire. Protection, abundance.
- coriander—Mars, fire. Fresh coriander (leaf) protects against evil.
- cumin—Mars, fire. Protective.
- dill—Mercury. Digestive, protects children. Fresh dill was believed to drive away evil.
- garlic—Mars. Protective, hex-breaking, health-giving, anti-vampiric.
- ginger—Mars, fire. Love, money. Cleansing. Vibrant energy.
- horseradish—Mars, fire. Protective. Aids digestion. The 'bitter herb' of Passover.
- marjoram—Mercury, air. Encourages tranquillity.
- mustard—Mars, fire. Protection, courage.
- nutmeg—Jupiter. Don't overdo it—a pinch is enough. Too much can cause vomiting.
- parsley—Mercury. Protection—chefs used a parsley garnish originally to keep the Devil away. Parsley bath draws money (Creole).
- pepper, black—Mars. Protection, purification, banishing.
- peppermint—Mercury, air. A drop of peppermint oil in coffee is a great wake-up call.
- rose—Venus. Devotion, hearts-ease. Rosewater, petals in salads, rosepetal jam.
- rosemary—Sun, fire. Sacred to the Goddess, used in victory garlands. Assists memory.
- saffron—Jupiter. Bounty, leadership, prosperity.
- sage—Jupiter. A digestive, its proper name *Salvia officinalis* refers to its healing properties.
- thyme—Venus. Thyme tea sweetened with

honey—sip while visualising yourself in a satisfying relationship.

- turmeric—Mercury, air. Add to curries. Purificatory.
- vanilla—Venus. Love, sexuality. Wear it as a perfume! MUST be the real thing—most vanilla 'essence' is artificially flavoured.

Food for Festivals

The Celts (and their gods) were and are great ones for a party. Good food, plenty to drink, good company and conversation, and lots of music is the Celtic definition of Heaven. The eight festivals that make up the Wheel of the Year provide an excellent excuse (as if one needed an excuse) for regular partying.

There are lengthy and boring arguments about whether one should celebrate according to the Northern or the Southern wheel. At this stage, I suggest you pick a festival that looks interesting, and choose your menu accordingly. See Chapter Nine for further information.

- ***Samhain*** (31 October, Hallowe'en) is the Celtic New Year. In the Northern Hemisphere, animals which are unlikely to make it through a harsh winter are slaughtered and their meat eaten fresh, or preserved by salting and/or smoking. Late apples are gathered in and stored. Roast pork with apple sauce is a food choice for Samhain. Try the Harvest Heaven recipe for sweet potatoes to accompany the pork, or a baked ham, and draw abundance in with every mouthful.

- ***Yule*** (Winter Solstice) is the time when the day is shortest and night is longest. It's the perfect time for venison casserole and sesame potatoes. Drink the returning Sun's health in spicy mulled wine.

- ***Imbolc*** is a festival of the returning light in Britain. The Church celebrates Candlemas for the same reasons and in much the same way—by lighting candles. The word *imbolc* means 'ewe's milk'. Eat white foods—cheese, potatoes, chicken. An old-fashioned cheese-and-potato pie—layers of potato, sliced onions and cheese in a deep casserole, cooked with milk or cream—is a North of England tradition for this cold and snowy time. In Australia, of course, it's still summer, so ice-cream, Money Trifle and cold chicken may be more appropriate.

- ***Eostar*** (Spring Equinox) Nights and days are equal in length and Summer is on its way. Spring foods are eggs and all green and leafy vegetables. Try *colcannon* to celebrate this festival in Celtic style.

- ***Beltaine*** (1 May) was one of the great celebrations. A time for marriages, handfastings, and general concupiscence. Celebrate it in Australia when asparagus and strawberries are at peak perfection. Chocolate is the perfect food to celebrate the coming together of the Goddess and the God, Venus and Mars.

- ***Litha*** (Summer Solstice) coincides with a southern hemisphere Christmas. Make a Summer Solstice Delight pudding for your friends, and enjoy the Aphrodisian pleasures of cherries and other soft fruits.

- ***Lughnasadh*** (Lammas) falls on 1 August. This is the time of the first reaping of the grain and the making of the first, sacred loaf from its flour. Bread, pies and pastries of all kinds should be the centre of a Lammastide feast.

Harvest Heaven sweet potatoes are also appropriate.

- ***Mabon*** (Autumn Equinox) is the last festival in the Celtic year, which begins again at Samhain. Days and nights are of equal length but the year is moving towards winter. This is the last gathering in of the harvest crops. Pumpkin soup, money-drawing curry and Celebration Rice will prepare you abundantly for the cold nights ahead.

The Tools of Kitchen Witchery

In Chapter Two I set out the general tools that a witch or magico may decide she or he needs. Kitchen witchery has its own implements.

- **Element of Air:** the whisk, wooden spoon, blender. Benchtop altar for food preparation. Intelligence to read a recipe, wit to enjoy the fun of cooking.

- **Element of Fire:** sharp knives! Blunt knives are more likely to slip and damage you than sharp ones. Your stove is the Altar of South, as Fire is the element of transformation. Courage to be adventurous in trying new foods and recipes.

- **Element of Water:** Cups, glasses, bowls. Having a good laugh with a friend. Going around obstacles—turning a fallen soufflé into a sweet omelette. All liquid ingredients. Taps and sink. The capacity to change, to let go and wash away what is in the way or no longer needful.

- **Element of Earth:** Serving platters, plates, chopping and breadboards. All solid ingredients. The halved apple as your pentagram. Your pantry and its contents. Homemade pickles, jams and preserves. Home-grown herbs, fruit and vegetables. Steadfastness in your desire to serve health-giving and delicious food as a spiritual and pleasurable service to the Goddess.

- **Element of Spirit:** the Cauldron of Ceridwen, the Grail 'out of which each man and woman might have that which most met their hunger and their need'. The kitchen as the Heart of the House.

And in the words of an old Celtic blessing,

May your hearth never lack a fire, nor
your children a bed
May your cauldron always be full and
your cup never empty
May your door always be open to the
hungry and the lost
And may you rest a full day in Heaven
before the Devil knows you're dead.

Chapter Eight

times and seasons: what spell, why, and when?

To everything there is a season
And a time to every purpose under
Heaven.
Ecclesiastes 3.1

At various points in this book I have suggested that a spell or a charm is likely to be most effective when chanted, made or charged at a particular phase of the moon or the year. I have talked about dark, waxing, full and waning moons, and the waxing and waning halves of the year.

These are the magical tides to which Shakespeare—who like many intelligent men of his day, had an interest in matters magical—may be referring in *Julius Caesar*: 'There is a tide in the affairs of men, which taken at the flood, leads on to fortune'. Magic is made easier if you utilise the natural ebb and flow of the astral tides in your spellcasting and charm-making.

If your need to cast a spell or make a charm is urgent, then go ahead. It is possible to phrase the charging spell to use the tide of the time in which circumstance forces you to work. In any case, we talk in wisecrafting about 'working between the worlds' where both time and space are merely human constructs. Magic is made in the astral world which is between time and space, the world of an infinitude of possibilities, of potentiality coming into manifestation.

But just as it is easier to row a boat in the direction of, rather than against, the flow of a current, so it is easier to cast spells of increase when the moon is waxing, or charms of banishing when it is waning. If it is possible to choose when to begin a new project, it will progress more swiftly during a waxing moon. If you are revising and rewriting, a waning moon is helpful.

Farmers have known about the influence of the phases of the moon on crops for centuries—indeed, for millennia. Before the onset of modern agribusiness, they planted, not only according to the season, but also according to the phase of the moon. Observation and the teachings of their elders told them, for instance, that leafy annuals—cabbage, lettuce, spinach, silver beet, most herbs—did best when planted in the moon's first quarter.

The second quarter of the lunar month was best for 'fruiting annuals'—those vegetables which you want to produce abundant seed, or where the seed-bearing organ of the plant is what is eaten. This was the time to plant beans, corn, pumpkin, tomatoes, capsicum, peas, eggplant and zucchini.

In the moon's third quarter, they observed that the moon was beginning to decrease in size and the life-force of the plant was returning to its roots. This was the best time to sow root crops—beetroot, potatoes, carrots, onions, garlic, parsnips. This was also the time to sow or strike perennials such as trees, shrubs, berries and vines—any plant that grows on after a period of winter dormancy and which depends for its health on a well-developed root system.

The fourth quarter was not a time for planting, but for weeding, destruction of pests, and general maintenance.

Transplanting seedlings was reserved for the first and second quarters of the moon. Pruning was done on a waxing moon to stimulate growth and on a waning moon to retard it. Many backyard gardeners working in the traditions of their homeland still observe these rules and customs. The abundance of their harvests is an indication of the practical advantages of the method.

Originally, everything was magical. Nowadays, magic is the science or technology that we no longer understand, or have yet to come to understand.

The phases of the Moon

It is possible to buy lunar calendars which will tell you the exact moon phase, together with the sign of the zodiac in which the moon stands at any time of the month. If you really want to get into high-tech magic, you may want to know whether, for example, the moon is waxing in Leo (for abundance work) or waning in Virgo (to get rid of bad habits). Any esoteric bookseller will usually have these calendars in stock.

Old-time farmers and witches, however, simply looked up in the sky to find out what phase the moon was in. In any case, the practice of observing moon phases was so ingrained that they knew the phase just as, nowadays, we have an 'instinctive' knowledge of the approximate time of day.

- **Darkmoon** (dark of the moon) is when no sliver of moon appears in the sky. It is the point of transition between waning and waxing, and like all transitions, the energies are powerful but sometimes erratic. A lunar calendar will give you the exact time of transition. It is very often at an hour when you're likely to be fast asleep, but if you're awake it is a powerful time to work magic.

Unless you're very sure of what you're doing, however, I'd generally recommend waiting until the first sliver of the crescent new moon has appeared in the sky. This is traditionally a 'lucky' time—turn over the money in your pocket and say 'Lady Moon, new moon, send me silver to my need'.

- **Waxing moon** is the period between the appearance of the first sliver of the new moon, and full moon. Any spells or charms intended to increase—abundance, health, love—are best worked in waxing moon. Much healing work is done at waxing moon. If someone you love—or you yourself—has been in poor health, this is the time to work to increase their vitality and ability to fight disease or recover from surgery.

A note on the ethics of healing for others.

Everybody has a right to his or her own illness. You do not know what lesson they have chosen to learn from it, or what kind of healing is appropriate. I have been taught that it is unethical and arrogant to do healing work on behalf of another person *unless they have specifically asked me to do so*. Don't assume you know what's best for them. The only exceptions I would make to this rule is when the sufferer is a small child unable to give informed consent (especially if you are the child's mother), or in case of accident or similar emergency, when your object is to buy time or ease pain for the injured person until the ambulance arrives.

- **Full moon** is when the moon is at her brightest, and the full disc is showing in the sky. The moon will appear to be full for about three days. A lunar calendar will give you the exact time of transition from waxing to waning moon.

Traditionally the full moon is the time when the Goddess grants wishes to Her followers. It is also a time to acknowledge blessings received, for feasting and celebration, for giving your crystals and jewellery a moon-bath, and for *drinking down the moon* to increase your psychic sensitivity and contact with the Goddess.

DRINKING DOWN THE MOON

✧ At the time of the full moon, take a cleansing bath to which you have added salt, hyssop and jasmine or gardenia essential oil. Put on clean clothes or a robe and go to a place from which you can see the moon (it will have to be a clear night, of course). Take with you a silver chalice or bowl and spring water. Place the chalice so that you can see the moon reflected in the water. Focus on the image until it fills the bowl of the chalice. Then hold the chalice up towards the moon and say:

Lady Moon, Lady Moon, grant me my wish
As I drink down your image, held in this dish.
Lady Moon, Lady Moon, let me share in your power
Help me grow stronger, hour by hour.

✧ Drink down the water in the chalice, and feel Her knowledge and power beginning to work in and through you.

◎ **Waning moon** is the period (of approximately 14 days) between full moon and darkmoon. It is a time for work to banish bad habits, to bind another from doing harm (bearing in mind that as you bind, so you are bound), and for doing healing work to diminish someone's illness or disease. This would be the time to work, for example, for someone who has cancer in order that the tumour may begin to reduce in size, whereas working for their recovery after surgery would be best done in waxing moon.

The last few days before the change of phase from waning to waxing is not a time to work magic unless you are very experienced and know exactly what you are doing. Use it to read, to think about what you have learned, and to rest. There is such a thing as magical indigestion! Treat this as the magical or astral equivalent of going on a juice fast to clear the system.

- **Blue moons** aren't as rare as the expression 'once in a blue moon' might lead you to think. A 'blue moon' occurs when there are two full moons in the same calendar month. It's possible because we work on a solar rather than a lunar calendar, so if a full moon occurs on the first or second day of the month, there's just time (28 days) to sneak in another one before month-end. It's still an occurrence rare enough to be special. There was, for instance, one blue moon in May 1999, but there will be none in the year 2000.

  A blue moon is a time to do something special—self-dedication or initiation, for example. Or simply take time to drive into the country or to the coast, and watch the moon rise—alone or in the company of like-minded friends. On one occasion a group of us went to a little mineral spring over which a hawthorn tree grows, and made music and sang songs in honour of the Goddess and the God. It is a time out of time. Celebrate it.

The Wheel of the Year

The Celts and their predecessors in the British Isles saw time as a wheel—or, more accurately, a spiral, since one never comes back to quite the same place—divided by eight great festivals. We know that the megalithic peoples of Britain observed the same festivals, because the major stone circles, which they (not the Druids) built, are oriented towards seasonal markers which are the same for both Celt and pre-Celt. Castlerigg circle in the Lake District is oriented towards Imbolc sunrise. Stonehenge has markers for both Midsummer and Midwinter, and so on.

The Wheel of the Year is divided into eight seasonal festivals. The seasons are of course those of northern Europe, and specifically those of the British Isles. It is possible to transpose the festival dates to the southern hemisphere. For a number of reasons, I don't find this transposition very satisfactory, but I will give the dates for both Northern and Southern observance.

The Celtic year started on 31 October/1 November, and the Celtic day ran from sunset to sunset, so the festivals are often celebrated 'on the eve' of the day, in our terms.

- Samhain (Hallowe'en)—Northern, 31 October. Southern, 30 April.

- Yule (Winter Solstice)—Northern, 21–23 December* Southern, 21–23 June*. Shortest night of the year.

- Imbolc (Candlemas)—Northern, 1 February. Southern, 1 August. Festival of the Returning Light and of the Goddess as Brigdhe. Lambing time.

- Eostar (Spring Equinox)—Northern, 21–22 March*. Southern, 21–22 September. Spring flowers appear.

- Beltaine—Northern, 30 April/1 May. Southern, 31 October. Summer is a-coming in.

- Litha (Summer Solstice)—Northern, 21–23 June*. Southern, 21–23 December*. Longest day, shortest night.

- Lughnasadh (Lammas)—Northern, 1 August. Southern, 1 February. Reaping of the first grain.

- Mabon (Autumn Equinox)—Northern, 21–22 September*. Southern, 21–22 March. Gathering in the rest of the harvest.

* The exact date and time will vary. Consult an astrological calendar for precise times.

Even in Britain these dates are to some extent arbitrary, since (for example) Beltaine should be celebrated when the hawthorn (the May tree) is in full blossom. In the south of England, this might actually be on May Day, but in the north, it could be as late as the end of May. The celebration of Lammas depended on when the grain was ripe for harvesting. Again, location played a part, as well as whether it had been a good or a bad summer, and what the region's grain was—wheat in the south, oats and barley further north.

In a continent the size of Australia, the seasonal differences between, say, far north Queensland and Tasmania are so great as to make an arbitrary adherence even to the transposed Wheel pretty irrelevant. Work needs to be done on finding our own seasonal markers.

In southern Queensland, for instance, the marker for Beltaine (for me) would be the flowering of the jacaranda. The arrival of the Wet would have to be a significant marker in the far north and in cattle country. I would suggest that one needs to look at the true meaning, the mythic and archetypal significance, behind the seasonal festivals, and work out an Australian Wheel.

About the Festivals

Samhain, which in the Christian calendar falls on the eve of All Saints' Day (Hallowe'en), is a celebration, not of death but of the continuity of life. The Celts believed that life is ongoing—death is merely the point of transition from one stage of life to the next. So firm was their belief in the continuity of life that they were quite willing to lend money and contract debts on the understanding that the loan would be repaid in the next life. Since they also believed in reincarnation, the next life didn't necessarily mean *Annwn*, the after-life.

They also believed that the borders between the dead and the living were not rigid and impassible, but open for communication with the ancestors. This was especially so at Samhain, when experience and custom told them that the veil between the worlds became thinner. At such a time, those with the necessary skill and training could journey into the Otherworld to seek knowledge and guidance.

Samhain is the appropriate time to seek for advice on future actions. Ask for guidance to be given you in dreams, or simply be open to information coming to you from an unexpected quarter. This would also be a good time to have a Tarot reading (find someone whose ethics you trust, or contact the Tarot Guild of Australia) or to update or have drawn up your astrological chart.

Samhain is also the time for *scrying*. This traditionally is done using a darkened mirror, a bowl of water, or a candle flame to assist the transition to an altered state of consciousness. Some people can scry in their computer screen—very high-tech witchery indeed! I would advise a considerable degree of caution here—scrying may be easier at Samhain, but if you actually find yourself seeing pictures, you'll probably be scared witless.

Choose a less powerful time for your first attempt, and have a sensible friend present to ask you what you're actually seeing. You'll be so busy watching the action that you may not remember why you went there in the first place.

I hesitated to mention scrying at all—but somebody out there is going to have heard about it and want to try it. Be cautious, as you would be with any new piece of technology. I can say this quite objectively, since scrying is not a talent I have. On the other hand, I *have* had to sit up all night with someone too frightened to go to sleep because of what they've seen.

Yule is the great Midwinter festival, taken over by Christianity as Christmas. It is the festival of the birth of the Child of Promise, who has been known in many cultures by many names—Jeheshua, Baldur, Mithras, Dionysus, Arthur. It celebrates the Return of the Sun, the rebirth of life and light and hope. This is a time for giving thanks and giving presents, for abundance-consciousness and making spells and charms to encourage abundance-consciousness during the waxing half of the year.

Imbolc is celebrated as a fire festival, welcoming back the returning light. The Church celebrates it as Candlemas, which has the same significance. It is also called Brigid or Brigdhe (Bride), who was a goddess long before she was a saint. It is a time to cast spells and make charms to increase light and clarity in your life.

Eostar—Spring or Vernal Equinox—is when night and day are of equal length, but the tides are moving steadily towards the bright light of summer. Like its opposite on the other side of the Wheel, Autumn Equinox, this is a time to work for balance in your life—while recognising that any balance is only temporary, because 'She changes everything She touches, and everything She touches, changes'. Celebrate the renewal of life in field and flower, and consider what the renewed light shows you in the darker and neglected corners of your psyche.

Beltaine—May Day—is actually celebrated on the eve, 30 April. In the myth cycle associated with the Wheel of the Year, this is the marriage of the Goddess and the God. Maypoles and hawthorn garlands bear out the phallic and yonic symbolism. For obvious reasons, this is the best time for love magic. It can also celebrate the inner union of the animus and the anima (to use the Jungian term) or help us work to balance the masculine and feminine aspects within ourselves. It's also traditionally a time for handfasting—the year-and-a-day marriages that the Celts very sensibly recognised as a good trial period before making the social commitment of raising a family.

Litha—Summer Solstice—is the festival of the Sun's power, the longest day of the year. After this point, however, the year begins to wane. A good time to look at what brings light to your life and to think how you can nurture it, and yourself, as the darkness approaches.

Lughnasadh—Lammas—is the beginning of the harvest. The first corn is reaped, the first, sacred loaf is baked, and the King begins his journey towards the Underworld. It is a time of mixed celebration and sorrow—rejoicing at a good harvest, sadness for the good things of Summer that will soon be gone. Spells and charms to do with coming to fruition, harvesting the benefits of work previously undertaken work well now.

Mabon—Autumn Equinox—is the time of final harvest. Time to take stock of what has served you well and what perhaps has not. Time also to look at what may need repairing (friendships, family relationships) before the dark comes.

The Wheel of the Year is at once a seasonal calendar, a myth cycle, and a journey of personal growth and exploration. It can and does work on many levels.

The Wheel as a seasonal calendar obviously works best if the dates of the festivals are reversed in their entirety. In Australia, it's clearly pretty silly to celebrate Yule as a midwinter festival in December, when the sun is riding high and the seasonal fruit and vegetables are singing summer. I've chosen (typical Gemini) to have a bet each way, and celebrate the solstices and equinoxes as they occur in the southern hemisphere, and the other festivals according to the northern calendar. None of this is written in stone. Find out what works for you.

The most important thing about the festivals, I believe, is that they give us markers in the year, times at which we make a conscious connection with the land and the seasons. These are times to celebrate and give thanks, in whatever way speaks to us, to the land that feeds and shelters us. It's a time to 'pay the rent'—plant a tree, tidy up your local creek bank, make an offering of milk or water (not alcohol), honey and grain to the land and to the spirits of the land. Whatever your race or background, this land supports and sustains you. Give it, and the spirits of the land, proper honour and respect, and your days and nights will be blessed, and joy will walk sweetly in your dreaming.

Postscript

towards the future

This has been a book about the simple, everyday magic available to us all. It is, if you like, the magic of the heart. It changes consciousness, but does so fairly gently, at a natural pace. It is, after all, *natural* magic, based on the seasons, cycles, elements and objects that make up the natural world.

For many people, this is as far as they want or need to go—at least, this lifetime round. It is enough to feel in harmony with the natural world, part of Nature's cycle of growth and renewal. The practice of wisecraft and earthmagic above all re-establishes our connection with our ground of being, the planet, Gaia, Terra.

But there is a world of knowledge and spiritual voyaging awaiting exploration—if you have the will to begin the journey and the courage to persist until you reach far landfall.

In the Bibliography you will find some books for your journey. There are many, many others.

In recent years there have been millions of words written about the old ways and the Old Religion. There have also been films, plays, television series, computer games, and—for all I know—interactive multimedia extravaganzas. Some have been frankly meretricious (look it up in a dictionary—as magical a volume as you'll find anywhere!), some merely superficial. Some are thorough, ethical, informative and very good indeed. Choose wisely, and don't accept everything you read (or see) at face value. That includes this book!

Test what you read and what you do against a simple yardstick. Does this path or this action help me to function more effectively in the everyday world? Does it help me to be kinder, more compassionate, more understanding in my relationships with others? If you cannot answer with an honest and resounding YES!, then ask yourself if it is the right path or action for you. It's also important to look at your own motivations. The path may be valid, but your reasons for walking it may need further examination.

Doubtless there are readers and viewers for whom wisecraft, witchcraft, the Pagan path is a bit of a giggle, a piece of naughtiness, a poke in the eye for society in general and the olds (their churchgoing parents) in particular. And for some, spells and charms offer (they think) a shortcut to power and control.

But there is far more to Paganism than spells, charms, candles and chanting. For me and for many like me, it is a religion—as serious a spiritual path as Buddhism, Islam, Christianity or Judaism. It is also older than any of them. It is the Old Religion of pre-Christian Europe.

The cave paintings of Lascaux and Les Trois Frères in France show the Horned God, or a shaman portraying him, as Lord of the Dance. The Venus of Willendorf is one of the earliest images we have of the human female expressing the glorious fecundity of the Goddess, Mother of All Living. Down through the ages, until belief was forced underground in the Burning Times, the men and women of Europe and the British Isles have worshipped the Divine as a duality—the Goddess and the God, equal in honour and respect, different in function.

We speak in ritual of 'She who sings in the heart and He

who dances'. We tell the story of the Descent of the Goddess into the Underworld in search of her lost love, and of her finding him there, transformed into the King of that realm. And we tell of how, for love of her, he surrendered his sword and crown, which she made into a circlet, the symbol of renewal and rebirth. And in love he entered into her, and in love he was reborn into the world once more. For there be three great mysteries in the life of humankind—birth, and death, and the renewal into life once more—and love controls them all. Love is the Law, and love the mystery.

THE CHARGE OF THE GODDESS

✦ Listen to the words of the Great Mother, who of old was called Artemis, Astarte, Dione, Melusine, Aphrodite, Ceridwen, Diana, Arianrhod, Brigid, and by many other names:

Whenever you have need of anything, once in the month, and better it be when the moon is full, you shall assemble in some secret place and adore Me who is Queen of all the Wise. You shall be free from slavery, and as a sign that you be free, you shall be naked in your rites. Sing, feast, dance, make music and love, all in My presence, for Mine is the ecstasy of the spirit and Mine also is joy on earth. For my law is love unto all beings. Mine is the secret that opens the door of youth, and Mine is the cup of wine of life that is the Cauldron of Ceridwen that is the holy grail of immortality. I give the knowledge of the spirit eternal, and beyond death I give peace and freedom and reunion with those that have gone before. Nor do I demand aught of sacrifice, for behold, I am the Mother of all things, and My love is poured out upon the earth.

✦ Hear now the words of the Star Goddess, the dust of whose feet are the hosts of heaven, whose body encircles the universe:

I who am the beauty of the green earth and the white moon among the stars and the mysteries of the waters, I call upon your soul to arise and come unto me. For I am the soul of nature that gives life to the universe. From Me all things proceed and unto Me they must return. Let My worship be in the heart that rejoices, for behold—all acts of love and pleasure are My rituals. Let there be beauty and strength, power and compassion, honour and humility, mirth and reverence within you. And you who seek to know Me, know that your seeking and yearning will avail you not, unless you know the Mystery: for if that which you seek, you find not within yourself, you will never find it without. For behold, I have been with you from the beginning, and I am that which is attained at the end of desire.

Doreen Valiente

THE CHARGE OF THE GOD

✦ Hark and pay heed to the words of the Old Horned One, who is ever young, ever renewing:

I am he who opens the doors of life and death,
The gates of dawn and the gates of night.
I am Gatekeeper and Guardian, the Watcher on the Threshold
Protector of the Goddess, my love and my lady,
And of all women, Her garments and jewels.

I am Kernunnos, and Silvanus, and Pan,
And the music of my pipes is in the air
Of the green woods and upon the summer hills.

My voice is in the wind of midnight
And the hawk's cry, and the bellow of stag in rut
And beneath the stars it speaks words of magic
In ancient tongues forgotten and unknown.

I am Lucifer the Light-Bearer, and Amoun the Hidden One
Who bore the spiral horns of the ram in ancient Khem.

I am the goat-foot God in the sunlit groves of Thessaly,
The presence that was felt in the darkness of the sacred cave,
And by the standing stones upon the heath.

I am Dionysus. Lord of Wine and laughter
And sweet unreason is my song in grove and stony height
And I am Apollo, Sun-Lord and healer
Whose law is measure in all things,
And who bids you know yourself, 'gnothi se auton'.

I am the God who greets the Goddess
With snowdrops at Imbolc, her friend and brother
And I am he who in laughing strength
Joins her at Beltaine as lover and spouse.
In summer I warm her and swell in her belly
And at Lammas am harvested and fall with the corn.
She seeks me at Samhain in my kingdom belowground
And finds me, and loves me, and renews me again.
I am Arthur and Baldur, Osiris and Mithras
The Sun-Child of promise born at Midwinter
I am hero and scholar, seeker of wisdom
Lover and friend and husband and brother.

I am the onrushing power of Life
And the bearer of Light; but without Love
I can create nothing that endures.

Therefore I need the Goddess, my Lady
As She needs me, Horned One, Dancer
And in the Sacred Marriage, the dance of being and becoming,
We two are one, heart and mind and soul.

So hear me now as I give you My charge:

Honour all women, for they are Her garments
Tread lightly on the earth, for it is Her body
Speak gently, secure in your strength and power
And celebrate life, and love, and laughter
In whatever way gives you joy and pleasure.
An it harm none of my Lady's creation,
Do what thou willst shall be the whole of the Law,
For Love is Her law, and Love Her mystery.

Doreen Valiente and Cassandra Carter

Or as St Paul wrote in another context: 'faith, hope, and love, these three—but the greatest of these is love'.

Go well, travel hopefully, and reach safe harbour. Or as we say at the end of a Circle meeting:

The Circle is open but unbroken.
May the peace, and joy, and love, and good fellowship of the Lady and the Lord,
She who sings in the heart and He who dances,

Be with you, now and always.
Merry meet, merry part, and merry meet again.
The work is done, the rite is ended.
There is a blessing on all who serve.

glossary

Amulet Symbolic object (e.g. the Eye of Horus, the Pentacle), often worn as a pendant or carried on the person, which is believed to have the power to avert misfortune or bring good luck.

Animus/anima Jungian terms for the male and female aspects of the soul.

Ankh Egyptian symbol of eternal life, associated with the Goddess Isis.

Athame Black-handled ritual short blade used to *cast the circle* and focus energy in magical work. Tradition says that it should be a double-edged blade. In Celtic tradition it (and its big brother, the sword) are symbolic of the will, forged in the fires of courage.

Aura The layered force-field around the physical body. It is connected with the vortices of force known in Eastern esoteric anatomy as the *chakras*.

Boline The name given in Gardnerian and Alexandrian witchcraft to the white-handled knife, often with a bronze blade, used to gather herbs. The word may have the same derivation as 'baleen', a type of whale whose bones were used in corsetry and cutlery making.

Book of Shadows The name given in modern witchcraft to a record or journal of rituals, spells, ingredients used in assembling charms, and similar material. The rituals are sometimes claimed to be secret knowledge handed down in unbroken line since the Burning Times!

Call a Quarter, to See **Quarter**.

Cauldron of Ceridwen Pre-Christian symbol of renewal and rebirth in the Celtic tradition Medieval Christianity gave many of its attributes to the Holy Grail of Arthurian legend. Ceridwen is the name given in the Welsh tradition to one of the faces of the Goddess, at once all-giving and all-consuming.

Chakra A Sanskrit word which means 'wheel'. The name given in Eastern esoteric anatomy to one of a number of vortices (some texts say as many as 108) which draw energy into the physical body.

Chalice A stemmed goblet, often of silver, which symbolises the feminine and the Element of Water in ritual work. A *yonic* symbol.

Chant A phrase or series of words (e.g. 'She changes everything She touches', 'Morgan, Morrigan, Macha, Bedbh, Ceridwen, Brigid, Medbh') repeated in order to alter consciousness, raise energy and focus intent. The power so raised may be used to empower a charm, perform healing or other magical work, and/or change the state of consciousness of the chanter(s). From the same root word as *charm* and enchanter.

Charge To imbue (e.g. a *charm*) with magical power.

Charge of the Goddess Paean of praise to the Lady and Mother, Creator of all that was, and is, and will be, the dust of Whose feet is as the hosts of Heaven, Whose body encircles the Universe. An important part of Gardnerian witchcraft rituals, its composition is generally attributed to Doreen Valiente.

Charm See **chant**, and text throughout.

Circle Used as a term or title for a magical working group, usually practitioners of earthmagic who choose not to call themselves a *coven* See also **Lodge**.

Circle, to cast To create sacred space for ritual work, particularly in earthmagic, with reference to the Elemental Powers. Ceremonial magicians are more likely to refer to 'raising the Temple' or 'opening the Lodge'. See also **Quarters, calling the**.

Coven Term used to describe a group of people (witches, bishops) gathered or called together for a religious purpose. From the same Latin root as 'convent' and 'convene'.

Covenstead The house in which a *coven* meets on a regular basis, if they are unable to work outdoors.Usually the home of the group's leader, but if another coven member has a larger space, the group may meet there. The term is not usually applied to a public meeting hall.

Cross of the Elements The equal-armed cross, often called the Celtic cross. The four points or arms represent the Four Elements, with Spirit placed at the centre, at the crossing-point of the arms. Often shown enclosed in a circle, the symbol of both eternity and rebirth.

Darkmoon I use this of the time immediately after the change of phase from waning to waxing, before the first sliver of the new moon has appeared in the sky. Dark of the Moon, the alternative usage, can be taken to mean the period before the change of phase—traditionally a time for negative or banishing magic. See Chapter Eight.

Dress (an altar) To prepare it for ritual work by placing on it an altar cloth, candles, symbols of the Elements, ritual tools etc.

Dress (a candle) To anoint it with a perfumed oil in preparation for candle magic.

Elementals Orders of beings embodying and carrying out the functions of the Four Elements. Each order is ruled by an

Elemental King. Sylphs (element of Air) are ruled by Paralda. Salamanders (element of Fire) are ruled by Djinn. Undines (element of Water) are ruled by Nixsa. Gnomes (element of Earth) are ruled by Ghob. More a feature of ceremonial magic than of Celtic wisecraft, which tends to work more directly with the *Elements*.

Elements, the Four Air, Fire, Water and Earth. In human psychology they represent the qualities of intelligence, courage, feeling and endurance; or wit, will, joy and steadfastness. The fifth element, the ruler and reconciler of the other four, is Spirit.

Esbat The monthly meeting of a witches' coven. It takes place at the time of full moon. The word probably comes from the Old French *s'esbattre*, meaning to frolic and amuse oneself. See also **Sabbat**.

Eucharist Holy Communion, the sharing of bread and wine in memory of the Last Supper.

Feng shui Name given to Chinese geomancy which employs principles of harmony and balance in the layout of house, garden and landscape.

Four Worlds, the Qabalistic concept describing the levels of reality from the most dense *(Assiah)* through *Yetsirah* and *Briah*, to *Atziluth*. Each of the Four Worlds contains its own *Otz Chaim*, the Tree of Life.

Gaia The name given by James Lovelock and others to the planetary intelligence. From Greek mythology, in which Gaia is the Mother of All, the Goddess before the Gods.

Ghee Clarified butter used in Indian cooking. Because the cow is sacred in Hindu culture, food cooked in ghee is deemed especially 'prasad', sanctified or blessed.

Grove Druid equivalent of a lodge. Refers to both the place and the group who meet there. So 'He (or she) is a Druid of Grove Arianrhod'.

High Mass Celebration of the *Eucharist* with emphasis on formal ceremony—procession, asperging the congregation, use of incense in a *thurible*, plainchant, and a musical setting of the key points of the Mass (Kyrie, Sanctus, Agnus Dei, Gloria, Benedictus). Sometimes called (by the less reverent) 'smells and bells'.

High Self The non-physical part of each individual which is their direct channel of communication to and with the Most High. Not the same as the soul, which it however encompasses, and beyond personality. That which survives from life to life and which will at the end of days be reunited with the Most High, the Light beyond the light.

Holy Guardian Angel Another name for the High Self. Conversation with the Holy Guardian Angel is one of the aspirations of ceremonial magic. It may also be one of the titles of Metatron, the archangel of *Kether* in *Briah* (see **Four Worlds**, **Qabalah**, **sephira/sephiroth**).

Kamea The name given to the *sigil* appropriate to a particular planet or archangelic force. It is devised using a system of squares linked with Qabalistic numerology. Used in ceremonial magic rather than wisecraft.

Karma Eastern concept sometimes simplified as 'what goes around, comes around'. Also used to mean fate, predestination. The Law of Karma states that you get back what you give out, though the balancing may take a number of lives. Known in wisecraft as the Law of Threefold Return—what you send out, whether for good or ill, will return to you threefold. Instant karma (the Cosmic Wet Fish factor) doesn't hang around for a future life, but operates for your better instruction in this one.

Lamen Term used in ceremonial magic to refer to the magical token or *amulet* worn over the heart chakra during ritual.

Lodge Term used in ceremonial magic to describe a place of working, as well as the group of people who gather there on a regular basis. Generally speaking, a dedicated space which is not used for any other function—e.g. a Masonic lodge.

Magico My term for a person generally interested in and a practitioner of the Arts Magical—it covers everyone from Wiccans to Druids, Freemasons and Qabalists. It does not include practitioners of *legerdemain* or other forms of stage magic. In the USA it has become common to use the old spelling of 'magick' to distinguish the real thing from stage magic.

Mojo bag A bag, often of velvet or leather, used to hold tumbled stones, crystals, herbs etc—items believed to hold particular power or virtue for the person carrying them. Possibly Creole, the term, originally used exclusively by practitioners of Voudoun and Santeria, has moved into more general American Wiccan usage.

Ouija board A circular board with the letters of the alphabet around the rim, used to receive messages from the departed. A most unreliable (and sometimes unsafe) method of communication. Let the dead sleep sweetly, and trouble not their dreams.

Pentacle The five-pointed star (the Star of the Goddess), enclosed in a circle. As a wooden platter or copper disc, the pentacle is used as a symbol of the Element of Earth in ritual. Sometimes spelt *pantacle*.

Pentagram The five-pointed star, as drawn at each Quarter in ritual invocation of the Elements. Common in Wicca, but Celtic wisecrafters often use the *Cross of the Elements* or the much older form of the spiral when *calling a Quarter*.

Qabalah The name given to the Jewish system of magic and mystical teaching which dates back at least to medieval times. Originally taught and learned exclusively by oral methods and memory—the word is usually interpreted as meaning 'from mouth to ear'. A complex set of ideas and analogies, Qabalah cannot be summarised in a few lines. Its basic concept, the Tree of Life *(Otz Chaim)* is encapsulated in a glyph setting out the *sephiroth* through which the Creator has manifested into the material world. An entire system of correspondences is based on the *sephiroth* and their planetary attributions. Qabalah (also spelt Kabbalah and Cabala) is the foundation of most systems of ceremonial magic.

Quarter Term used to indicate the direction (east, south, west, north) from which power and protection is drawn into a ritual or into the ritual area.

Quarter colours The colours associated in my tradition with Air (yellow), Fire (red), Water (blue) and Earth (dark green). The candles which mark the Quarters are usually in the Quarter colours. The Spirit candle is usually purple, violet or white. Note that other traditions use other colour attributions. All are equally correct.

Quarters, to call the To invite or invoke the presence of the Powers into sacred space prior to ritual work.

Reserved Sacrament The unconsumed portion of consecrated wafer remaining after celebration of the *Eucharist*, often kept in a specially designated chapel or a box on the altar. For Christians who believe in transubstantiation, the Reserved Sacrament is an object of particular sanctity, since the act of consecration has transformed it into the Real Presence—the body of Christ.

Sabbat The general name for any one of the major festivals on the eightfold Wheel of the Year. See Chapter Eight. The Sabbats are sometimes divided into the Greater Sabbats (Imbolc, Beltaine, Lughnasadh and Samhain) and the Lesser Sabbats (the equinoxes and solstices). Doreen Valiente devotes several fascinating pages in her *ABC of Witchcraft* to Sabbat origins and customs.

Salmon of Wisdom Figure in Celtic mythology. In Welsh myth, the Salmon of Wisdom lives in a pool overhung by nine hazelnut trees (a Goddess symbol), on the nuts of which it feeds. Undoubtedly related to the salmon cooked by Finn MacCoul in Irish myth.

Samhain Celtic New Year, All Hallows Eve. See Chapter Eight.

Scourge A nine-thonged whip used in Gardnerian and Alexandrian witchcraft initiations.

Scrying Seeing the future by gazing into a reflective (or non-reflective—whichever works for you) surface such as a pool of ink, darkened mirror, crystal ball or computer screen. Fire (a bonfire or a candle flame) is also sometimes used.

Séance A 'sitting' at which the dead are asked for advice, the location of missing articles (jewellery, a will) or similar, through a medium or use of a *ouija board.*

Sephira/sephiroth *Sephira* is singular, *sephiroth* is plural. The stations on the Tree of Life (see **Qabalah**) representing various stages of manifestation of the Creator. There are ten *sephiroth* (eleven including *Da'ath*), each of which has its own planetary attribution, Archangel, choir of angels, colour, sound and number (to name but a few). Since there are also *Four Worlds,* in each of which stands a Tree of Life, the potential for complexity is enormous. The word itself means 'sapphire' or 'shining'.

Sigil An occult sign or device supposed to have mysterious powers. From the Latin *sigillum*, a seal. See *kamea.*

Spell Word-magic.

Spellbox A small, usually wooden, box originally (and correctly) used to hold the ashes of the paper or vellum on which a spell has been inscribed. The ashes were later disposed of in the Samhain bonfire. Now more commonly refers to a box used to hold an inscribed spell until the spell has come into effect, or one used to keep spellcasting materials in.

Tabard A loose surcoat open at the sides, sometimes worn over ritual robes as an indication of a person's office or function within a *Lodge* or particular ritual.

Talisman In general usage, the term is applied to a good-luck piece. Since Renaissance times it has also described a stone, ring or other object engraved with characters to which are attributed the occult powers of the planets or other forces they represent. Metal or parchment are now more commonly used the inscribe the relevant *sigils.*

Thurible A vessel in which incense is burnt in religious ceremonies. Now usually made of brass, with a pierced lid to allow the incense to escape. The lid also keeps the hot charcoal safely inside when the thurible is swung to cense a place or congregation. For private use, a pottery dish filled with sand (to absorb the heat from the charcoal) is perfectly adequate and much less expensive.

Tincture The alcohol-based extraction of the active principle(s) of a herb.

Trine Astrological term defining a particular, usually beneficial, planetary alignment in which two planets are separated by 120 degrees.

True-name The secret name by which you are known to the Gods and possibly your spiritual teacher, if you have one Often given to you in meditation.

Votive 'Given'. Votive candles are the small candles used in Catholic churches to draw the attention of a saint or the Blessed Virgin to a prayer.

Wand A straight, slender stick. Does not need to have a star on the end.

Yonic. Adjectival form of *yoni*, Hindu for the female genitals. The opposite of phallic.

suppliers and resources

This is a short list of who supplies what, and where to find them. The Victorian suppliers are ones I know and deal with personally. Interstate suppliers are listed on recommendations.

Adyar Bookshop, 230 Clarence St, Sydney, NSW 2000. Tel (02) 9267 8509. Website: www.adyar.com.au; e-mail: inquiry@adyar.com.au

Auroma, 86 Burwood Rd, Hawthorn, VIC 3122. Tel (03) 9818 2673 (showroom), and 39 Melverton Drive, Hallam, VIC 3803. Tel (03) 9796 4833 (warehouse orders). e-mail: auroma@ozemail.com.au
Website: www.auroma.com.au/

Source of professional-practitioner quality pure essential oils, from angelica to ylang ylang—about 250 in the current catalogue. They also sell aromatherapy blends, carrier oils, bodycare products, gums and resins (such as frankincense), botanicals, fragrances and potpourri oils. The range is huge. Price and stock list available on request, or check out their website. They do a lot of mail order business, so if you don't have easy access to a reliable supplier of pure essential oils, these are the people to contact.

Book and Crystal Den, 87A Hannan St, Kalgoorlie, WA 6430. Tel (08) 9091 3288.

Circling Winds, Shop 18–19, 99 Elizabeth St, Brisbane, Q 4000. Tel (07) 3221 8436.

Cosmic Pages, 338–340 King William St, Adelaide, SA 5000. Tel (08) 8231 9105, (08) 8231 6720.

Down to Earth Bookshop, 790 Hay St, Perth, WA 6000. Tel (08) 9321 9752.

Esoteric Bookshop, Glen Arcade, 675 Glenferrie Rd, Hawthorn, VIC 3122. Tel (03) 9818 1998. Website: www.esotericbookshop.com.au

'Spells—we have the stuff they're made of' is their slogan and they're not kidding. The place to find everything from High John the Conqueror root to Van Van oil. If they don't have it they'll find it for you. Also a good range of amulets, and a selection of ritual tools (athames, swords, pentacles), essential oils, and candles. Will take orders for robes and cloaks. And, of course, they have esoteric books—a remarkable range in such a small space. (I think they've mastered the Tardis spell.) Free catalogue. Mail order service available. Always helpful to the novice.

Healing Hands Holistic Health, 10 Vine St, Clayfield, Q 4011. Tel (07) 3256 1567.

Kimberley Bookshop, 4 Napier Tce, Broome, WA 6725. Tel (08) 9192 1944.

Mysterys, First Floor, 314 Darling St, Balmain, NSW 2041. Tel (02) 9818 2274.

Occult supplies, botanicals etc. Mail order catalogue.

Nature's Workshop, 348 Separation St, Northcote, VIC 3070. Tel (03) 9482 2677. Fax (03) 9481 1393.

Complete range of crystals (from amethyst geodes to smoky celestials) and tumbled stones (carnelian, aventurine, malachite, turquoise etc). They also carry potpourri ingredients (rosebuds, lavender, oakmoss), some essential oils, jewellery, and a small range of books and CDs. Their notice board is always worth a look.

Quantum Books, 113 Melbourne St, North Adelaide, SA 5006. Tel (08) 8267 1579.

St Peter's Church, Eastern Hill, Albert St, East Melbourne, VIC 3001.

In my opinion, the best Anglo-Catholic smells-and-bells in Melbourne. A Solemn High Mass here is a lesson in High Magic ritual, beautifully staged. Even if you're not usually a churchgoer, go to one of the major festivals—Midnight Mass on Christmas Eve, for instance. The music here is an especial delight—everything from Palestrina to Haydn.

St Peter's Bookroom, tel (03) 9663 7487.

Attached to St Peter's Church. Their candles are very good value, available in a wide range of sizes, and twenty-five per cent beeswax. Also a source of charcoal and a range of Church incenses (Prinknash, Three Kings). They also have good-quality greetings cards, icons (the church has an Icon School), and a range of books on Christian topics.

The Sandalwood Factory, 218 Nicholson St, Fitzroy, VIC 3065. Tel (03) 9416 4366. Website: www.mtromance.com.au

Suppliers of excellent Australian-grown sandalwood products (including pure sandalwood incense and oils) and a good range of aromatherapy oils and natural beauty and skincare products.

Soul Food, 273 Smith St, Fitzroy, VIC 3065.
Tel (03) 9419 5347

They stock a vast range of dried herbs, from the culinary to the medicinal. This is the place to find hyssop, damiana, coltsfoot and mugwort, amongst many others, sold by weight from large jars. Soul Food is primarily a health food shop (rather than an esoteric supplier), but its range of goods and its fresh produce section makes it one of the best in Melbourne. The shop will supply herbs and spices by mail order (arrangement by prior phone call requested).

Southern Cross Church Supplies, 608 Glenferrie Rd, Hawthorn, VIC 3122. Tel (03) 9818 5166.

Vestments of great gorgeousness, incense, charcoal, thuribles, candles (they carry pillar candles in the Quarter colours)—and the Monastique range of cosmetics. Will supply by mail.

Spiral Books, 269 Smith St, Fitzroy, VIC 3065.
Tel (03) 9417 2576.

Just down from Soul Food—a good reason for making a special trip. New Age, Goddess spirituality, psychology, children's books and healing are their special areas of interest, but they carry a good range of handmade candles, incense (sticks), aromatherapy oils, cards and music. Extensive range of esoteric/symbolic silver jewellery. They also often have Tarot readers available—phone first to make a booking.

Theosophical Society Bookshop, 126–128 Russell St, Melbourne, VIC 3000. Tel (03) 9650 3955.

Together with its sister bookshop, Adyar Books in Sydney, it has the largest range of esoteric books in the southern hemisphere. Everything from Sai Baba to Crowley. Comprehensive range of Tarot cards, as well as incenses, candles and oils. They also carry Aura-Soma oils and essences. Worth checking out their second-hand section for the odd gem. Mail order service is quick and efficient.

Wisdom Books, 432 Hay St, Subiaco, WA 6008. Tel (08) 9382 2817.

OTHER RESOURCES

G.R.A.I.L. (Goodwill Resource And Information Listings) Directory, PO Box 1444, Canberra City, ACT 2601.

A slim but very useful volume giving contacts for reputable groups, courses, newsletters, magazines etc. Cooperatively published by APIC—the Australian Pagan Information Centre, PO Box 300, Australian National University, Acton, ACT 2601.

Tarot Guild of Australia, PO Box 369, East Kew, VIC 3102. Tel (03) 9859 7355.

Tarot courses, workshops, training and certification offered. Contact them to find a reputable Tarot reader in your area.

Witchcraft magazine (published by FPC Magazines, 180 Burke Rd, Alexandria, NSW 2015, obtainable from newsagents).

Carries advertisements for a range of suppliers and specialist bookshops and services in most states.

OVERSEAS CONTACTS

Chalice Well Trust, Chilkwell St, Glastonbury, Somerset BA6 8DD, United Kingdom. Tel (01458) 831154.
Website: www.chalicewell.org.uk

The Trust takes care of Chalice Well (one of the oldest Holy Wells in Britain), maintains the gardens, runs a small bookshop, and publishes 'The Chalice', a newsletter for the friends and supporters of the Trust and its work. Chalice Well is a place of deep peace and healing, and the Goddess breathes Her blessing over it. Even in midwinter, with snow on the ground, the gardens remain beautiful. If you become a Companion of the Well, Little St Michael's self-catering accommodation can be booked for a retreat and respite from the world.

New Moon Occult Supplies, PO Box 110, Didcot, Oxon OX11 7YH, United Kingdom.

Mail order only, but everything the Compleat Magico could possibly desire, and then some. Check out their website at www.newmoon.uk.com

Order of Bards, Ovates and Druids (OBOD), PO Box 1333, Lewes, East Sussex BN7 1HB, United Kingdom.
Website: www.obod.co.uk/obod

Offers a full training program through the three grades of Druidry. A distance learning program offers lessons, audio cassettes and a monthly magazine. OBOD runs regular retreats and camps, with a strong emphasis on the environment and the arts. Definitely check them out if planning a trip to the UK.

Osiris, 19 Heath Rd, Twickenham, London TW2 4AW, United Kingdom.

The full pantheon of Egyptian godforms, beautifully made

and exclusive to Osiris. Also a range of classical (Graeco-Roman) statuettes and other artwork. Catalogue is available—but send an A4 envelope and International Postal Reply coupon with your request.

Pagan Federation of Great Britain, BM Box 7097, London WC1N 3XX, United Kingdom.

Website: www.paganfed.demon.co.uk

The umbrella organisation for Pagans of various persuasions, from Druid to Wicca to Asatru. Publishes a quarterly magazine, Pagan Dawn, which has very good articles and reviews on matters of Pagan interest. Especially useful if you're planning a trip to the UK and Europe and want like-minded contacts. Their annual conference, in November, is well worth going to if you're in the UK at the time.

Servants of the Light, PO Box 215, St Helier, Jersey, Channel Islands, United Kingdom.

Website: www.servantsofthelight.org

Dolores Ashcroft-Nowicki is the Director of Studies of this Association, which offers a full course of esoteric studies in the Western Mystery Tradition, by correspondence but under individual supervision. Primarily Qabalist and ceremonial in orientation, but there are plans afoot to offer specialist courses (e.g. in wisecraft, esoteric healing, etc) once primary training is complete. SOL traces its lineage back to Dion Fortune's Fellowship of the Inner Light, and through them to the Order of the Golden Dawn. Particularly strong on the Egyptian mysteries.

ON THE NET: SITES OF INTEREST

witch.drak.net/sunnette (Down Under Pagan Resource Centre)

www.wiccaworld.com.au (Australian Wiccan, Pagan and Occult Supplies)
www.e-witch.com (e-witch Pagan Auction site)
www.maxpages.com/motherwitch (Motherwitch Circle site)
www.spiritualnetwork.com (a pagan search engine)
www.grandmother-spider.com (book reviews of major authors and thinkers of the 'Earth Spiritual Community')
www.petand.demon.co.uk (Eco Pagan News)
www.witchvox.com (The Witches' Voice: A News & Education Network)
www.paganfed.demon.co.uk (The Pagan Federation Online)
hometown.aol.com/wiccanware/Wiccanware/index.html (clothes etc for 'Magickal people')

Wicca chatrooms
www.egroups.com/group/30Wiccans
www.wiccanway.net

sources and further reading

Ashcroft-Nowicki, Dolores, *The Ritual Magic Workbook*, Aquarian Press, 1986

Ashcroft-Nowicki, Dolores, *First Steps in Ritual*, Aquarian Press, 1990

Ashcroft-Nowicki, Dolores, *The Tree of Ecstasy*, Aquarian Press, 1991

Ashcroft-Nowicki, Dolores, *Daughters of Eve*, Aquarian Press, 1993

Ashcroft-Nowicki, Dolores, *The Shining Paths*, Aquarian Press, 1983

Assagioli, Roberto, *Psychosynthesis: A Manual of Principles and Techniques*, Aquarian Press, 1990

Assagioli, Roberto, *The Act of Will*, Wildwood House, 1974; Penguin, 1987

Beyerl, Paul, *The Master Book of Herbalism*, Phoenix Publishing, 1984

Bolen, Jean Shinoda, *Goddesses in Everywoman*, Harper Colophon, 1985

Bolen, Jean Shinoda, *Gods in Everyman*, Harper Colophon, 1989

Brennan, Barbara Ann, *Hands of Light*, Bantam Books, 1988

Brennan, Barbara Ann, *Light Emerging*, Bantam Books, 1993

Butler, Ernest, *How to Read the Aura*, Aquarian Press, 1979

Conway, David, *Secret Wisdom*, Aquarian Press, 1987

Conway, David, *The Complete Magic Primer*, Aquarian Press, 1988

Cooper, J.C., *An Illustrated Encyclopaedia of Traditional Symbols*, Thames and Hudson, 1984

Crowley, Vivianne, *Wicca: The Old Religion in the New Age*, Aquarian, 1989

Cunningham, Scott, *Cunningham's Encyclopaedia of Magical Herbs*, Llewellyn Publications, 1989

Cunningham, Scott, *Cunningham's Encyclopedia of Crystal. Gem and Mineral Magic*, Llewellyn Publications, 1988

Cunningham, Scott, *The Magic in Food*, Llewellyn Publications, 1990

Davidson, Gustav, *A Dictionary of Angels*, Free Press/Macmillan, 1971

Denning & Phillips, *Psychic Self-Defense & Well-Being*, Llewellyn Publications, 1994

Ellis, Normandi, *Awakening Osiris*, Phanes Press, 1988

Farrar, Janet and Stewart, *Eight Sabbats for Witches*, Robert Hale, 1981

Farrar, Janet and Stewart, *The Witches' Way*, Robert Hale, 1984

Ferrucci, Piero, *What We May Be*, Turnstone, 1982

Fortune, Dion, *Psychic Self-Defence*, Aquarian Press, 1984

Fortune, Dion, *The Mystical Qabalah*, Samuel Weiser, 1983 (first pub. 1935)

Glass, Robert, *From the Goddess* (tape and CD)

Gonzalez-Wippler, Migene, *The Complete Book of Amulets and Talismans*, Llewellyn Publications, 1991

Graves, Robert, *The White Goddess*, Faber and Faber, 1984

Greer, Mary K., *The Essence of Magic*, Newcastle Publishing Co. Inc., 1993

Howe, Ellic, *Magicians of the Golden Dawn*, Aquarian Press, 1985

Huebner, Louise, *Power Through Witchcraft*, Nash Publishing, 1969

Judith, Anodea, *Wheels of Life*, Llewellyn Publications, 1987

Knight, Gareth, *A Practical Guide to Qabalistic Symbolism*, Helios Books, 1976

Kunz, G. F., *The Curious Lore of Precious Stones*, Bell Publishing, 1989 (facsimile edn)

Lawlor, Robert, *Voices of the First Day*, Inner Traditions, 1991

Lee, W.H. and L., *Herbal Love Potions*, Keats Publishing Inc., 1991

Matthews, Caitlin, ed., *Voices of the Goddess*, Aquarian Press, 1990

Miller, R.A. and I., *The Magical and Ritual Use of Perfumes*, Destiny Books, 1990

Regardie, Israel, *The Art of True Healing*, New World Library, 1991 (first pub. 1932)

Richardson, Alan, *Earth God Rising*, Llewellyn Publications, 1990

Richardson, Alan, *An Introduction to the Mystical Qabala*, Aquarian Press, 1991

Skelton, Robin, *Spellcraft*, Phoenix Publishing Inc., 1998

Skelton, Robin, *Talismanic Magic*, Samuel Weiser Inc., 1985

Slade, Paddy, *Diary of a Village Witch*, Capall Bann, 1997

Starhawk, *The Spiral Dance*, Harper and Row, 1979 (Revised and extended 1989, 1999)

Tansley, David, *The Raiment of Light*, Arkana, 1984

Telesco, Patricia, *A Kitchen Witch's Cookbook*, Llewellyn Publications, 1998

Valiente, Doreen, *An ABC of Witchcraft*, Phoenix Publishing, 1988

Wang, Robert, *Qabalistic Tarot*, Samuel Weiser, 1983

Weinstein, Marion, *Positive Magic*, Phoenix Publishing, 1986

WitchCraft Book of Spells, magazine, various contributors, n.d.

Worth, Valerie, *The Crone's Book of Words*, Llewellyn Publications, 1986

Zimmer, Thomas, *Astrological Calendar and Moon Planting Guide*, large-format wallchart published annually. Obtainable at esoteric bookshops or direct from the author at Mount Cougal Road, Tallebudgera Valley, Queensland 4228.